ARMED AMERICA

BOOKS BY ELAINE LANDAU

CHILD ABUSE
An American Epidemic

DIFFERENT DRUMMER
Homosexuality in America

THE HOMELESS

ON THE STREETS
The Lives of Adolescent Prostitutes

TEENAGE VIOLENCE

TEENAGERS TALK ABOUT SCHOOL

WHY ARE THEY STARVING THEMSELVES?
Understanding Anorexia Nervosa and Bulimia

ARMED AMERICA

THE STATUS OF GUN CONTROL

ELAINE LANDAU

Julian Messner

Published by Julian Messner, a division of
Silver Burdett Press, Inc., Simon & Schuster, Inc.
Prentice Hall Bldg., Englewood Cliffs, NJ 07632

JULIAN MESSNER and colophon are trademarks of
Simon & Schuster, Inc. Design by Michael J. Freeland
Manufactured in the United States of America.

Lib. ed. 10   9   8   7   6   5   4   3   2   1
paper ed. 10   9   8   7   6   5   4   3   2   1

Library of Congress Cataloging-in-Publication Data
Landau, Elaine.
Armed America : the status of gun control / Elaine Landau.
p.   cm.
Includes bibliographical references and index.
Summary: Discusses the problems caused by Americans' arming
themselves and presents a case for gun control.
1. Gun control—United States—Juvenile literature.   2. Violent
crimes—United States—Juvenile literature.   3. Firearms ownership–
United States—Juvenile literature.   [1. Gun control.
2. Firearms—Law and legislation.]   I. Title.
HV7436.L36   1990
363.3'3'0973—dc20   90-40238
ISBN 0-671-72387-1 (trade)   CIP
ISBN 0-671-72386-3 (LSB)   AC

For Norman

CONTENTS

ARMED AMERICA

AMERICA'S

ARSENAL

It happened on one of those beautiful sunfilled days California is known for. Approximately 450 grade school children from Cleveland Elementary School in Stockton, California, had left their classrooms to enjoy midday recess in their schoolyard. Most of the children ranged in grade level from kindergarten through third. Involved in their playground games, no one seemed to notice the 26-year-old man dressed in combat fatigues as he made his way to the schoolyard.

The man was Patrick Purdy. As a child he had also attended Cleveland Elementary School, but today he'd returned on a twisted mission. When he reached the schoolyard area, Purdy lifted his Chinese-made AK-47 assault rifle to his shoulder and opened fire on the unsuspecting students. There'd been no warning, and the children had little opportunity to take cover. As bullets flew, the screams of injured and frightened young people filled the air.

A witness later noted that Purdy hadn't appeared angry as he fired; he merely seemed to be concentrating on his aim as he mowed down the children with speed and precision. His one-man massacre was over within moments. After spraying the playground with more than 106 bullets, Purdy pulled a pistol from his jacket. This time, he pointed the weapon at his head and pulled the trigger. The bullet entered his skull and Purdy died immediately. His was not the only life lost that day. Patrick Purdy's actions resulted in the deaths of five young people between six and nine years of age. In addition, 29 other children and a teacher were wounded.

The investigation following the incident revealed that Patrick Purdy was an alcoholic drifter who had previously been arrested for attempted robbery and selling weapons. He'd demonstrated a fascination for militaristic assaults and weaponry. In his room, police found toy soldiers, which some

Mourners pray over the caskets of some of the Cleveland Elementary School students who were shot by Patrick Purdy in 1989.

mental health experts suspect Purdy might have manipulated for weeks in a sort of bizarre mental rehearsal of the schoolyard massacre.

The weapon Patrick Purdy used on the young children was a high-powered semiautomatic rifle—once regarded as a weapon of war. Although semiautomatics release only one bullet with each trigger pull, these guns are capable of firing large rounds of ammunition as the trigger is repetitively squeezed. The weapon's effects may be devastating. Due to the rifle's tremendous velocity, the shock waves reverberating from its bullets can shatter body parts that haven't been directly hit. Even from a distance, a spray of bullets discharged from a semiautomatic is sufficiently powerful to make a concrete wall look like Swiss cheese. These guns frequently destroy human organs to the point at which they cannot be repaired by doctors. There's no chance of setting bones that have been pulverized.

For example, in describing a patient brought to a hospital after being shot on his right side, a resident surgeon stated that, ordinarily, only some slight damage to the patient's liver should have resulted. However, since the victim had been shot with a semiautomatic rifle, his kidney, aorta, pancreas, diaphragm, and liver had been destroyed. Twenty-five units of blood were needed as doctors diligently tried to piece their patient together during surgery. An additional 40 units of blood products were used in the next 24 hours prior to the patient's death.

Doctors who treat assault rifle injuries often claim they practice "trench medicine" and refer to their hospitals as "MASH" units. Indeed, the similarities to battleground injuries are chillingly real. As Dr. Garen Wintemute, an assistant professor of medicine at the University of California and former medical director of a refugee camp in Cambodia, stated: "The medical techniques used in the Vietnam War are now being used in civilian life. There's no difference. And this wasn't the case until the advent of assault rifles."[1] In some areas, the situation has become critical. In fact, at least one hospital in Los Angeles has offered its emergency room as a training ground for Army surgeons.

Semiautomatics differ from automatic machine guns in that while a semiautomatic requires that the trigger be squeezed for each bullet released, fully automatic guns have the capacity to fire hundreds of rounds of ammunition with a single trigger pull. Both types of weapons are frequently referred to as assault rifles. Many semiautomatic rifle models can easily be converted into fully automatic machine guns. Although modifying a weapon in this manner is illegal and carries penalties as severe as a 20-year jail term and a $20,000 fine, in some instances the transformation may be brought about as easily as inserting a nickel or match stick into the weapon.

Yet semiautomatic machine guns have a tremendous capacity for the destruction of life just as they are. At one time these fast-firing weapons were rarely used outside of the military. However, once relations were normalized between

A semiautomatic rifle with a collapsible shoulder piece.

the United States and China, in 1979, the importation of Chinese goods became legal. The Chinese AK-47 Patrick Purdy used on the elementary school children in Stockton, California, proved to be among the most popular Chinese imports.

American weapons manufacturers anxious to exploit the high demand for the gun designed copies of the lethal AK-47. Sales of the domestically manufactured copies soared as well. While 4,000 AK-47 copies were sold in 1986, over 40,000 were purchased in 1988.[2] Other types of semiautomatics have also proven to be highly salable among American gun consumers. Indicative of the rising appeal of semiautomatic weapons are the skyrocketing sales of the MAC-10—a relatively inexpensive American-made semiautomatic. Perhaps equally popular is the semiautomatic AR-15, which was modeled after the U.S. military M-16 infantry rifle.

Presently, a number of states prohibit private ownership of fully automatic machine guns. In other areas, a 1934 federal law has made it extremely difficult for anyone besides the police, the military, and licensed gun collectors to buy these weapons. In these instances, applying for both the mandatory federal and state machine gun permits may be a lengthy and cumbersome process. However, the opposite is generally true in purchasing semiautomatics. In fact, in some states it may be easier to obtain these guns than a driver's license.

To purchase a semiautomatic machine gun, an individual need only show proof of being over eighteen years of age and a United States citizen. He must attest to the fact that he is not a convicted felon and has never been confined or jailed for drunkenness, drug addiction, or mental illness. No fingerprinting or background check is required in many states. Often would-be semiautomatic purchasers need only fill out a few forms and bring sufficient cash to leave with the weapon. That's how Patrick Purdy bought his AK-47 in a gun shop in Sandy, Oregon, for $350.

In determining appropriate guidelines to regulate the use of these weapons, the question frequently arises as to which private citizens would want or need a gun with such deadly firing capacity. Unfortunately, police departments throughout urban America are well aware that semiautomatics are now the weapon of choice among inner-city drug gangs.

Brutal displays of deadly force have become an accepted by-product of the growing crack industry. Due to its formerly exorbitant price, cocaine had largely been available only to the affluent. Once crack became readily available in $5.00 vials, however, this cocaine derivative became affordable to the poor as well as to those of means. The mass marketing of crack created a present day drug industry worth tens of billions of dollars.

Drug profiteers hurriedly set up shop on the street corners and in the housing projects of poor neighborhoods, where crack could be purchased by both individuals of means and impoverished ghetto residents. The seemingly limitless demand for this highly addictive drug resulted in unprecedented dealer profits. Controlling sales turf became synonymous with wealth, and gang members were prepared to employ the most powerful weaponry possible to prevent interlopers from infringing on their territories.

The intensive firepower of semiautomatics has been instrumental in helping drug lords and their regimes to blast away any threat to their self-proclaimed dealing territories. Unfortunately, in addition to rival gang members, their targets have also included police officers and innocent bystanders. The innocent bystanders wounded or killed in drug-related shoot-outs are referred to by gang members as "mushrooms." The number of blameless individuals killed by gang gunfire in New York City, Boston, Los Angeles, and Washington, D.C., tripled between 1986 and 1989.[3] One 33-year-old Washington, D.C., woman was killed in a blast of crossfire as she sat on her porch, trying to catch a breath of fresh air on a warm summer's day.

Authorities cite a direct correlation between the infusion of crack dealers in urban areas and the subsequent rise in popularity of semiautomatic weapons. Sadly, at times the parallel is all too vivid. In some areas, flashes of gunfire from armed gangs engaged in shoot-outs are commonplace. The sight of dead bodies being carried away, distraught families, and burned-out cars has begun to lose its shock value as these images become characteristic of a growing number of poor areas. What was once a neighborhood may now look like a combat zone.

The magnitude of firepower used by drug gangs is often difficult to comprehend. Recently, the Chicago police "gun-buster" unit raided a West Side gang's headquarters. Among other weapons, the officers found eight machine guns, seven sawed-off rifles, a semiautomatic rifle, twenty handguns and thousands of rounds of ammunition. Some of the drugland shoot-outs may seem unnecessary and even border on being reckless. Drug gang members have often been described as trigger happy. Such self-destructive tendencies may be somewhat enhanced by the fact that many drug traffickers use crack themselves. The feelings of paranoia (delusions of persecution) induced by the drug may serve to further dissolve the inhibitions usually associated with deadly weaponry. As a result, these individuals are more likely to find themselves in a kill-or-be-killed situation.

Unfortunately, the use of deadly force appears to have had a somewhat trickle-down effect on other types of criminals as well. While in the past burglars and car thieves were generally unarmed or equipped with relatively crude firearms, today the scenario has dramatically changed. Police now report a marked tendency for all types of criminals to carry firearms as well as to engage in gun play rather than submit to arrest. As an officer of the Houston, Texas, police force described the situation: "Just about everybody committing a crime has a gun. Not cheap Saturday night specials, but guns they can count on. And they're willing to shoot them rather than go to jail."[4]

The inclination toward armed violence is evident in young people as well as in those with lengthy criminal pasts. Students have shown up at junior high schools carrying semiautomatics as well as an assortment of other guns. On some New York City street corners, an 11-year-old can purchase a revolver for as little as $25. Criminal arms dealers will often lend out a weapon for an evening or two. This way a young person is afforded an opportunity to raise sufficient cash through muggings and robberies to actually purchase the gun of his choice. According to one psychotherapist from Sacramento, California: "Guns seem to be enjoying a new chic. The increased prevalence of gun carrying among students is reflective of an increased general interest in guns in this country."[5]

The ultimate result of this increased tendency to be armed is that in many parts of America, police forces are now outgunned by criminals. For years, the standard police weapon was the six-shot .38 caliber service revolver. However, an officer armed in this manner wouldn't stand a chance against a converted semiautomatic capable of firing 900 rounds of ammunition a minute. If the officer wasn't hit with the first slew of bullets, he'd surely be struck while he stopped to reload his revolver.

In response to this frightening reality, police have had to upgrade their weapons in order to remain competitive with the criminal element. In a number of urban areas, police units have discarded their .38 service revolvers for semi-automatics. The Drug Enforcement Administration (DEA) has begun arming its agents with a miniature submachine gun especially designed for this law enforcement agency by Colt Industries (gun manufacturers). The gun, known as the Colt SMG, is an extremely powerful weapon. Yet it's small enough to remain concealed beneath an agent's coat.

However, in some instances, arming law enforcement authorities with more powerful weapons may still not equal the odds. At times, some urban neighborhoods may seem uncontrollable. In these situations, the criminals may have better access to manpower and weapons than the police assigned to protect the area. In such war-zonelike regions, an officer who aggressively tackles the job at hand might easily be wounded or killed in the line of duty. Police may be hesitant to enter some buildings with fewer than five back-up officers, as they've been made painfully aware of the heavy-duty artillery they'll be facing.

A growing number of law enforcement professionals have openly stated that police units may no longer be able to combat the problem unassisted. There's been talk of the need for intervention by federal troops. Officials in New York, Los Angeles, and Washington, D.C. have requested that the National Guard be called in to assist in patrolling heavily crime-ridden areas.

Other attempts to defend against the rise in violent criminal behavior includes the development of more sophisticated weaponry, as was shown by exhibitors at a three-day police security exposition in Atlantic City, New Jersey. Among the weapons featured was the fearsome Striker-12. Although this shotgun is only 12 inches long, it has a six-inch barrel. As its distributor, Dick Delong, described the gun, "It's so awesome looking the perpetrator is more likely to surrender. He doesn't know what's going to come out of it, a laser beam, anything. The police would use these for close-in work, like [raiding] crack houses."[6]

The Striker-12 is capable of firing 12 rounds of ammunition with a single squeeze of the trigger. It is equipped with an optional day-night sight to allow officers to keep both eyes open while focusing on a target.

Also on display at the expo as another possible purchase for police departments was a six-wheeled lightweight vehicle called the Pinzgauer Ibex. The vehicle, designed with a .50 caliber machine gun affixed to its top, holds eight officers and is capable of ascending a stairway. The vehicle's bottom is encased in a steel covering to provide protection from possible mine attacks. The Pinzgauer Ibex ranges in price from $170,000 to $200,000, depending on the amount of equipment and extras the purchaser desires.

Meanwhile, in less obvious ways, the need to be armed in an increasingly violent society has even filtered down to honest law-abiding citizens. Newspapers are filled daily with accounts of violent confrontations in which innocent passersby are injured or killed. Nightly TV news programs often dramatically portray the fate of crime victims who were unprepared to defend themselves.

Previously, the majority of American gun owners purchased their weapons for hunting or such sporting purposes as target shooting. Today, however, many Americans want a gun for protection. They feel unable to depend on the police to protect them from armed intruders breaking into their homes or confronting them in deserted areas as they walk to their cars at night.

Many survivors of violent crimes are determined not to be helpless if they're attacked again. This reality is underscored by the fact that an overwhelming number of guns have been purchased in urban areas, even though traditionally, more guns were bought for sporting purposes in rural areas of the South and West.

Is there a new breed of gun owner emerging? If so, then there are strong indications that women figure prominently among this population. A Gallup poll for Smith & Wesson (gun manufacturers) revealed that between 1983 and 1986, the number of female gun owners rose 53 percent. The same survey indicated that nearly four times as many women as had been polled in the past (nearly two million) were then contemplating purchasing a gun. Updated figures on how many of these women actually bought weapons are not available, though it is likely that at least some may have.

The women who own guns in America today span a broad range of occupations and age levels. Some are barely out of their teens, while others are of retirement age. While some hold high-ranking executive positions in the business world, many of these women pride themselves on being home-makers. The increase in female gun ownership may be somewhat indicative of a rejection of stereotypical gender roles. In many ways, modern day women have traded a traditional reliance on men for opportunities to better learn to defend themselves. Numerous women who've grown tired of continually looking over their shoulder in an increasingly violent environment have chosen to become gun owners.

In response to this fairly new and growing market, gun manufacturers have begun to design weapons that they hope will be especially appealing to women. This has resulted in the creation of designer weapons—new lightweight guns that can be easily concealed in attractive purses with holsters

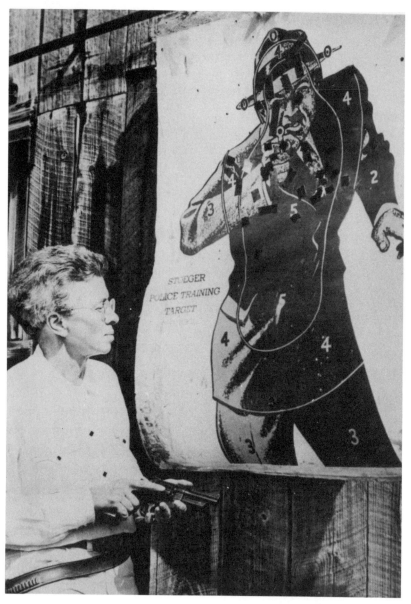

Numerous women have started buying and carrying guns. This woman is practicing shooting at a target.

from companies such as the Bang Bang Boutique and Feminine Protection. The industry has even sponsored gun and fashion shows to demonstrate the many ways to carry a weapon without having it detract from a fashionable appearance. In one show, a swimsuit-clad model revealed how a woman could easily conceal a lightweight gun within her hair bow. Another marketable item is a "how to" video on buying and trying firearms. The tape, which has reached record sales, is primarily geared for female audiences.

Some women who have recently bought firearms claim that they haven't regretted their purchases. One such individual had been involved in her company's computer operations and was required to be at work by 5:30 a.m. At that early morning hour most of the streets surrounding her office building were deserted. The first time she was mugged by three young men, she'd fought to hold on to her purse. The police later explained to her that that was probably why she'd been so badly beaten by her assailants. She was advised to simply hand over the desired articles if she were ever involved in a similar incident.

Therefore, three months later when she was again stopped by the same group of men, she willingly gave up her money and jewelry. Apparently, her lack of resistance made little difference to her attackers. She was beaten, thrown to the ground, and repeatedly kicked. This time, the results of the assault were even more devastating than before. The woman suffered a broken jaw and two broken ribs.

At that point, she reasoned that the same three men probably roamed the seemingly abandoned streets at that hour, seeking out defenseless prey. The woman inquired about altering her work schedule to enable her to travel with the rush hour crowd. However, the nine-to-five shift paid considerably less, and at the time she couldn't afford a cut in pay.

Following her recovery, the woman's brother escorted her to work for several weeks. However, he had a job as well as other responsibilities, and the early morning routine of picking up his sister, accompanying her to work and then putting in a full day at his own office proved to be too taxing. That was when the woman decided to purchase a gun. She needed her job but felt she could no longer remain vulnerable to the random attacks of criminals. As she said:

"A few years ago owning a gun would have been unthinkable to me. I hated guns and thought that only hunters, criminals, and nut cases owned them. But that was before I had my jaw broken for nothing other than a sick young man's sadistic pleasure. I hope I never have to use it. I hope I never see those guys or anyone like them again. But I'm physically no match for the three of them, and I can't go on being their victim. I can't continue to wake up every morning feeling afraid and never knowing if I'll make it to work that day."

As it turned out, she did meet those three young men again. The third time they approached her, one laughingly said, "What do you have for us this time?" Flashing the gun she had clutched in her coat pocket, she fired one shot into the air and yelled, "I've got *this* for you!" The three men immediately fled. They never approached her again, and fortunately she hasn't had call to use her weapon since that time.

Security experts attest to the fact that large numbers of people are presently increasing measures to protect themselves. More are hiring private guard services, installing better lighting and locks, and purchasing guns. According to a survey disclosed by the Justice Department, the combined totals paid by businesses and individuals for security measures surpasses the 22 billion in tax dollars annually allotted for police protection. A good portion of the money is used to purchase guns. For example, in Los Angeles immediately following a dozen break-ins and murders by a perpetrator known as "the night stalker," local gun dealers reported a soaring increase in weapons sales.

Although many Americans have chosen to arm themselves for self-defense purposes, owning a gun may not always be synonymous with knowing how to use one. Gun owners who rely on their weapons in confrontations with intruders or muggers sometimes find that the criminals are more adept at handling firearms than they are. At times, owning a gun may have cost these individuals their lives. In addition, many gun owners who have neglected to learn the proper use of their weapons have become involved in accidental shootings.

In an attempt to ward off such potentially lethal consequences, some new gun owners have made certain they are adequately trained through both instruction and practice time at the shooting range. There also appears to be a rising interest in a sport known as "practical shooting." Through the artificial creation of dangerous criminal scenarios, practical shooting allows individuals to test their reactions and abilities under high-stress conditions. Throughout the game or drill, both cardboard and metal humanlike forms unexpectedly pop up from behind doors, windows, and bushes. The practical shooters have only a moment in which to take aim and fire. Participants receive points for accurate shots and penalties for missing a target or shooting the wrong target—referred to as a "hostage" in some of the scenarios.

One practical shooting enthusiast who's won several national titles for her expertise is former Dallas Cowboy cheerleader JoAnne Hall. Ms. Hall became involved in the sport after completing a defensive shooting class in Dallas. As she described her feelings about these shooting exercises:

"The real benefits are that you become more confident and self-assured when you're home. You're less apt to make a mistake and shoot at shadows or a neighbor out of panic or fear."[7]

For some individuals, being prepared has paid off. In 1984 Arthur Stiles of Fort Ann, New York, had his home broken into by two burglars. The sum of $33,000 was stolen from his residence. One of the burglars was apprehended and served a year in prison for the crime. Three years later, the same man returned to the Stiles residence to commit another robbery.

The second time Stiles was robbed, he was ready to confront the intruders. Having heard them break into the house, Stiles stood armed as he waited for the men to enter the kitchen. As the intruders approached him, he fired his gun and wounded one of the men. This time, the same burglar who had previously broken into Stiles's home was sentenced to five to ten years in prison.

The number of weapons as well as the variety of guns available in America today is vast, and continues to grow as weapon technology becomes increasingly sophisticated. In addition to the criminal use of guns, the upscaling of police weapons, and gun ownership by private citizens for self-protection, Americans also purchase weapons for other reasons. Hunters and target shooters have long relied on guns for sporting purposes, while gun collectors admire the craftsmanship and design of firearms.

In some occupational settings other than law enforcement, carrying a gun has proven essential for survival. For example, one afternoon B. J. Schmitz, a biologist for the U.S. Fish and Wildlife Service, had been studying wild geese in their natural habitat, about 185 miles northwest of Fairbanks, Alaska. All of a sudden, Schmitz noticed that the geese had begun to stir.

Looking up, Schmitz spied a large grizzly standing only about 15 feet from where she sat. A moment later, the bear charged toward her. Schmitz quickly grabbed her shotgun and fired. She hit the grizzly in the head, killing the animal instantly. Later, in recalling the incident, B. J. Schmitz felt fortunate to be alive. "What if I hadn't had my gun?" she remarked.

Some individuals may have valid reasons for being armed, while others purchase weapons with criminal intent. Nevertheless, some sociologists feel that nothing short of a domestic arms race among United States citizens is presently underway. According to the Federal Bureau of Alcohol, Tobacco, and Firearms, Americans possess two to three million semiautomatic assault rifles. It's difficult to secure an accurate figure of how many people actually own guns, since many weapons are illegally obtained and, therefore, remain unregistered.

However, it's been estimated that over 60 million handguns and 40 million rifles are owned by 70 million United States citizens.[8] If all the guns presently owned in America were collectively gathered, it's likely that at least one weapon would be available for every adult and child in the United States.[9] Perhaps America is truly on its way to becoming an armed nation.

1. *The New York Times*, February 21, 1989, p. 1.
2. *Time*, February 6, 1989, p. 22.
3. *U.S. News & World Report*, July 31, 1989, p. 12.
4. *Time*, February 6, 1989, p. 23.
5. *Newsweek*, January 11, 1988, p. 18.
6. *The New York Times*, July 1, 1989, p. 27.
7. *Newsweek*, October 6, 1989, p. 28.
8,9. *U.S. News & World Report*, May 8, 1989, p. 22.

READY, AIM...FIRE:
A HISTORY OF
WEAPONRY

Since their invention, guns have been used for both heroic and brutal purposes. As a result, the history of firearms is both extensive and controversial. In the 1200s AD the Chinese invented black powder, which was also known as gun powder. By the 1300s, people realized that gun powder could be used to propel objects through the air. Word of this invention rapidly spread throughout Asia and Europe. The first weapon to be activated by gun powder was the cannon. However, as time passed, weaponry became less cumbersome and more efficient for individual use. Portable firearms that could be carried on one's person were developed.

Guns revolutionized the nature of warfare. While at one time battle armor protected its wearer from fatal lance blows, bullets could easily pierce a knight's thin metal shield. Castles, which had proven worthy fortresses against the blows of rocks, bows and arrows, and swords, were destroyed following continuous cannon assaults.

As weaponry design advanced, soldiers fought using pistols and muskets. These early weapons were often heavy and awkward. Muskets had to be loaded from the muzzle, which could be a time-consuming process. Nevertheless, guns proved to be significantly more efficient as killing instruments than either sharpened spears or bows and arrows. An important breakthrough in early firearm technology took place in the 1500s with the invention of the rifle. The later addition of spiral grooves within the gun's barrel served to make it the most precise firing instrument of that period.

Guns have always occupied a niche in the fabric of America's history and culture. Struggling colonists in the New World faced many dangers and hardships but were fortified by their weapons in their attempts to survive. A survey of firearms taken at the Jamestown, Virginia, colony in

During the Revolutionary War, American colonists took up arms to fight for freedom from Great Britain.

1624 indicated that the number of guns equaled the number of colonists present. Americans learned early on that guns were essential to their existence. Colonists used their weapons for hunting as well as for protection.

During the American Revolution, colonists took up arms to break free from British tyranny. Volunteers, organized into military companies, drilled for hours to sharpen their skills in aiming and firing weapons. Although many of these men might have been ordinary farmers, blacksmiths, and tradespeople, during the American Revolution they were known as Minutemen because they could be counted on to grab their guns and fight at a moment's notice.

The first attack by American Minutemen against British troops took place at old North Bridge near Concord, Massachusetts. Although only a few casualties on each side resulted from this encounter, these shots came to be known as "the shots heard round the world." Minutemen groups later fought alongside of the colonial militia and proved to be instrumental on the Revolutionary battlefield.

Throughout this period, a patriotic fervor filled the air. Colonists eagerly took up arms to help ensure a better life for their families and themselves. Some who seemed unlikely soldiers proved themselves skilled marksmen. Among those who heeded the call to arms was Henry Knox, a Boston bookseller who became a superb artillery man from techniques he learned from books. Nathanael Greene was a Rhode Island Quaker who agreed to take up arms for the righteous pursuit of freedom and liberty. Joseph Warren, a Boston doctor, boldly responded to British insinuations that the colonists lacked bravery and fighting skills when he proclaimed, "Those fellows say we won't fight. I hope I shall die up to my knees in blood!" Unfortunately, Warren proved his point all too well. He was killed in the Battle of Bunker Hill.

America was a nation born out of strife and revolution. Rather than viewed as tools of destruction, guns came to be seen as an important means of securing freedom and justice. Guns were so closely associated with liberty that the writers of the Constitution drafted the Second Amendment in 1791 as part of the Bill of Rights. The amendment states: "A well regulated Militia, being necessary to the security of a free State, the right of the people to keep and bear Arms, shall not be infringed."

The "weapons" amendment was heartily endorsed with a minimum of debate when the first Congress was held in New York City. It was supported by such notable men as Thomas Jefferson and Samuel Adams. Jefferson took tremendous pride in the personal gun armory he kept at his home, Monticello, in Virginia. Sam Adams was a native son of Massachusetts, a state now known for its stiff penalties for unlicensed weapons.

As the country continued to grow and pioneers moved westward to settle new lands, guns remained an essential survival tool. Streams of pioneers braved rugged and dangerous conditions as they strove to establish settlements as far west as the Mississippi Valley. These westward-bound settlers had to travel largely unencumbered. They needed to be extremely selective in the items they brought along. However, no westward pioneer would ever have dreamed of tackling the perilous journey without a rifle. The pioneer's gun allowed him to shoot game. Without this ready supply of food, it's likely that many pioneers would have perished from starvation. It was difficult to bring very much food along as it was certain to spoil during the extensive journey. In addition, the pioneer's rifle was his only protection against wild animals.

Guns were also instrumental in the many brutal confrontations between pioneers and Indians. The pioneers continued their westward movement, disregarding the fact that they wished to settle lands on which Indians had hunted, fished, and lived for centuries. In some instances, the government made treaties with the Indians, which guaranteed the Indians portions of these areas, but often such agreements were shortlived. Settlers anxious for still more territory used their superior weapons to overrun the Indians and seize their land, while the government stood by allowing the carnage to continue.

During the American Revolution, British troops supplied some Indian tribes with guns and encouraged them to fend off American settlers who were encroaching on Indian hunting territory. Guns, which have sometimes been referred to as "the great equalizers," enabled the Indians to hold their own for a time. Unable to contend with frequent attacks on their newly founded frontier settlements, some pioneers fled or were driven back East.

However, within a short period of time, large droves of settlers once again headed West. To defend against Indian attacks, they now built tall stockades of wooden logs behind which settlers sought temporary refuge from aggressive tribes. The stockades were designed with firing posts—slits in the log structure sufficiently large to allow a rifle to be thrust through. Men and even young boys who had already learned to handle a gun took turns standing guard at the stockades' firing posts. Although women usually kept those on guard supplied with ammunition, sometimes they were needed on the firing line as well.

Pioneers were self-reliant and used guns for hunting and for protection.

The Indians soon grew hesitant to attack the stockades. It was nearly impossible to survive a heavy barrage of rifle fire from an enemy shielded by a wooden blockade. Meanwhile, the westward movement of white settlers continued. Before long, the Indians found themselves outnumbered as well as outgunned.

As the years passed, pioneers moved further west in increasing numbers. However, many never reached their destinations. Only a small percent were killed by Indians. Instead, large numbers of men, women, and children died of cholera and smallpox. Shooting accidents were another major cause of death among pioneers.

Americans who went West were often forced to start their new lives in a lawless environment. The various laws and codes of ethics that had regulated public conduct in the East were no longer workable in the pioneers' new surroundings. Since these small western communities were frequently isolated and separated from one another by vast distances, law enforcement proved to be an especially challenging task. One sheriff might be responsible for protecting an area spanning more than 500 miles. Some towns were so new and poorly equipped that there wasn't even a jail in which to confine a captured criminal.

Even in places where there was a jail, an outlaw's friends or relatives might ride into town and terrorize the inhabitants, often shooting innocent bystanders until the culprit they came for was released. Perhaps the most famous judge in the West was Roy Bean. He held court in a Texas saloon, assisted in his administration of justice by only a slim law book and a loaded revolver.

Disputes involving cattle, a valuable ranching commodity, were common in the West. Before barbed wire came into use, cattle roamed freely on the open range. Rustlers frequently stole newborn and as yet unbranded calves. They also altered the brands of cattle belonging to others. Western justice was swift for cattle rustlers who had the misfortune to be caught. They were usually shot or hanged on the spot.

Still another source of conflict on the range were the disputes that broke out between cattle ranchers and farmers. The farmers didn't want the ranchers' cattle to graze on and roam through their planted fields. Arguments between cowboys and farmers were often settled by gun play. The winner was the man who wasn't carried out.

Perhaps the violence reached its zenith in Wyoming in 1892, during the Johnson County Cattle War. Cattle ranchers feuding with farmers over their cattle's grazing rights thought the farmers might be stealing their cows. Although they had no positive proof that their suspicions were correct, the ranchers drew up a list of farmers whom they felt might be involved.

The ranchers decided to resort to guns to permanently settle the issue. They hired 25 professional gunfighters from Texas to ride with 30 of their own men against the farmers. After two farmers were killed, their side took up arms to meet the challenge. Fortunately, federal troops became aware of the conflict and arrived in time to avert a bloodbath.

A good deal of violence has also been associated with the cattle towns of the Old West. A number of cow towns had sprung up at sites where the trail drives ended and railroads shipped the cattle to the East. Because cowboys and trail bosses were paid at the drive's end, they usually had ample funds with which to partake in the morally dubious activities a cattle town had to offer. Saloonkeepers, gamblers, and dance hall girls stood ready to part a cowboy from his hard-earned dollars. Since cardsharps, who cheated at poker, and other swindlers frequented these towns as well, many disputes erupted into violence. Arguments were often settled by gunfire; the loser did *not* get an opportunity to apologize.

Fictionalized stories and Hollywood movies have often depicted cowboys as gun-toting men who were excellent shots. In actuality, this wasn't so. Cowboys generally didn't like to wear a gun while working, as they spent much of their day on horseback, and a gun tended to add weight and bulk. However, cowboys did find guns useful on trail drives to turn back a cow stampede or kill a rattlesnake.

Although they knew how to fire their weapons, the typical cowboy could hardly be considered a quick draw. Also, cowboys tended to be quite young, and developing expertise in the quick draw required a good deal of practice. As these men were generally poorly paid, they usually couldn't afford the bullets necessary to improve their shooting skills. As a result, young cowboys were often no match for the more experienced gunmen they encountered in cow towns. Nearly every cow town had a cemetery named "Boot Hill" on its outskirts, where the victims of these unfortunate gun battles were laid to rest.

Mining camps of the West were also frequently characterized by violence and gun play. Often the lure of immediate wealth through striking gold drew a somewhat reckless type of individual to these camps. Miners who had "struck it rich" were sometimes mysteriously found shot to death, while others quickly laid claim to their stakes.

In countless instances involving gold and mining claims, guns continued to be equated with power and might. Armed bandits frequently robbed stagecoaches carrying precious metals to the East. A stagecoach driver surrounded by outlaws pointing their rifles at his head could most assuredly be counted on to hand over the booty. Outlaws, also known as desperados, often worked together in bands. Soon these gun-wielding groups expanded their realm of targets. In addition to attacking stagecoaches, they also robbed trains and banks.

The outlaws Frank and Jesse James, "the Dalton boys," and Billy the Kid became famous. Although gun play was an integral factor in the way they lived, many outlaws abided by their own code of honor. It was considered unmanly to sneak up on someone in order to shoot him in the back or to gun down an unarmed, defenseless person. Nevertheless, the outlaw's trigger finger robbed many innocent people of their lives. Although some desperados have been depicted as folk heroes, in actuality these men were little more than thieves and murderers.

Eventually, the West was tamed. Areas in which the fastest draw had once had the last word slowly evolved into peaceful, law-abiding communities. Disputes were now settled in courts of law, yet loyalty to the weapon that had helped the colonists win the Revolution and allowed pioneers to brave the frontier remained fervent. Guns were firmly rooted in American tradition. They had come to symbolize freedom, independence, and power—attributes that have often been used to describe America, a nation born and sustained with the help of gunfire.

Today, admiration for the gun and respect for its deadly power remains apparent in many aspects of our society. It is a potent force in the messages sent through film, television, and print media. For example, modern day "cowboys" were glorified in the form of detectives Crockett and Tubbs, stars of the television show *Miami Vice.* Hard rock music, hot-pink imagery, and expensive cars served as a backdrop for two ultracool cops who upheld the law with such heavy-duty artillery as futuristically designed semiautomatic machine guns. In the film *Rambo,* a patriotic Vietnam veteran relies on assault weapons to single-handedly free prisoners of war abandoned by a corrupt American bureaucracy.

Machine guns seem to have found a place in comedy as well. In the film *Who Framed Roger Rabbit?,* one of the "toon" detectives totes an automatic rifle while searching for Roger. Although cartoons have always been notoriously violent, the appearance of assault weapons added an especially contemporary flair.

Today's honest citizens don't think of guns as instruments for terrorizing others, but rather as a means of defending their lives, families, and property when law enforcement personnel aren't there to do so. Their thinking is reminiscent of that of the Western pioneer who used his rifle to protect his family from outlaws when the nearest sheriff resided a hundred miles away.

Even those who philosophically argue for stricter controls on weapons may still not readily relinquish the security afforded by a gun when faced by an attacker. One such incident occurred in 1989 when syndicated columnist Carl T. Rowan, a long-time advocate of strict gun controls, was awakened from his sleep by what he assumed was an intruder on his property. He called the police, then loaded his handgun and went outside to investigate the situation.

Rowan reported that moments later he was confronted by a "tall man who was smoking something that I was absolutely sure was marijuana." Rowan told the man to stay back, but when the intruder ignored the warning and continued to move toward him, Rowan fired once, wounding the man in the wrist.

Following the incident, his critics dubbed the columnist "Rambo Rowan" and similar nicknames. However, Rowan defended his actions as follows: "Let my political enemies crow. But let them know that as long as authorities leave this society awash in drugs and guns, I will protect my family."[1]

As incidents such as these become increasingly common, society is left to ponder an important question: Have guns become an inherent aspect of the American way?

---

1. *Time,* June 27, 1988, p. 58.

THE CASE FOR
BEING ARMED

Ellen (not her actual name) knew when she applied for her taxi driver's license that driving a cab could be dangerous. Yet it was the highest-paying job she could find, and she needed to save as much money as possible to return to college. The man she'd picked up from a late nightspot in the early hours of the morning hadn't seemed in any way unusual or suspicious as he hopped into her cab. She was, therefore, completely caught off guard when moments later he grabbed her neck from behind the seat.

The passenger held a broken bottle to Ellen's throat as he instructed her to drive out to a deserted area. After robbing her of the $70 she'd earned in fares that night, the man threw Ellen out of the cab and ordered her to crawl in the dirt. When he began walking toward her with the broken bottle clutched tightly in his fist, Ellen thought he was going to cut her throat. By then, she knew she had to act. Ellen took out the gun she had in her jacket pocket and fired at her assailant. He died in a hospital hours later. Ellen credits having a gun with being alive today.

Another incident involving an armed assault took place late one night during the Christmas season at a popular Birmingham, Alabama, eatery. Unfortunately, in this instance, it was the criminal who was armed. The diner owner had stepped out for a few minutes. An armed robber entered the restaurant, grabbed a woman customer, and held a gun to her head. Before the culprit's attack was over, another customer on the premises was shot in the neck.

The restaurant owner later regretted not having had his licensed .32 caliber pistol with him that night. He's since expressed his intent to purchase an M-1 rifle to attain maximum firepower if it's ever needed to protect the lives of his patrons and himself. He is not concerned that his being armed could possibly lead to further carnage. He refuses to wait as a ready victim for the next armed burglar and feels that being amply armed helps to equalize the odds when in conflict with others determined to do him harm.

There's a substantial constituency of individuals in the United States who are firmly against restricting gun ownership among law-abiding citizens. Many gun enthusiasts believe that Americans have a constitutional right to keep and bear arms, as guaranteed them by the Second Amendment to the Constitution. They feel that gun controls, or restrictions on arms, are merely infringements on the basic rights of American citizenry. These individuals believe that state and federal legislative attempts to restrict gun ownership are inherently unconstitutional. One attorney representing the views of gun enthusiasts stated that requiring gun owners to register their weapons is "like registering to exercise the right to free speech."[1]

Those in favor of private gun ownership often stress that at the time the Constitution was written, every able-bodied male was part of the militia. Therefore, the rights granted by the Second Amendment fully extend to all American citizens. This viewpoint contends that although statutes that disqualify convicted felons, drug addicts, and minors from owning guns are acceptable, preventing or placing obstacles in the path of law-abiding citizens who wish to purchase weapons is unreasonable.

As Dale Thurston of the anti-gun control group Citizens for a Better Stockton (California) stated: "If they [guns] were removed from us, we would discover why we need them, as the students in Red China recently found out. You need them in order to preserve freedom. When you lose them, you lose your freedom."[2]

Another common argument against gun control is that restrictive weapon laws will in no way deter criminals who can easily obtain their weapons illegally for illicit purposes. As former New York City Police Commissioner Patrick J. Murphy stated in response to the murder of a number of police officers while on duty: "Since eight of the nine guns used in the killings had been purchased illegally despite all the stringent anti-handgun laws already on the books in New York City, you have to wonder what good any further banning of handguns will do."[3]

Law enforcement officials have frequently cited how easily criminals have obtained the thousands of illegal handguns presently available. Despite Chicago's handgun laws, one federal agent has been quoted as saying that among the greatest risks in the high-crime districts of the city is that of having a gun fall on your head from a tall building as you walk down the street. Unfortunately, the ready availability of illegal weapons underscores the painful reality behind his attempt at black humor.

Those against gun control further argue that although gun restrictions would probably not greatly deter criminals, such legislation might have a detrimental effect on the ability of citizens to defend themselves against armed intruders. They believe that a criminal who knows a store owner has a gun behind the counter will probably be less likely to rob that shop than an establishment where he's certain that neither the proprietor nor the customers are armed. Gun enthusiasts fear gun control laws might inadvertently turn honest citizens into even easier targets for illegally armed criminals.

As Winnie Alphonse of the Coalition of New Jersey Sportsmen said in an interview with the author: "Just think about it. Would you put up a large sign on your door or in your window that read 'THERE ARE NO GUNS IN THIS HOME.'? If gun

Owners of businesses sometimes feel the need to own a handgun for protection. Pawnshops, like the one shown here, are often the source of inexpensive handguns.

control legislation outlawed the private ownership of firearms, you wouldn't need a sign. Criminals could rest assured that the storekeepers and home owners they wished to rob were unarmed. Even if you had a gun, your assailants would know that you'd hesitate to use it on them, because then you'd be in trouble for having illegally retained a weapon."

There's evidence to indicate that to some degree guns actually serve as a deterrence against criminal attacks. Sociologists James Wright and Peter Rossi conducted in-depth interviews with nearly 2,000 felons serving terms in various state prisons. Fifty-six percent of those interviewed indicated that they'd be significantly less likely to approach a potential victim who was armed, while 57 percent agreed that most criminals would rather meet up with the police than face a civilian with a gun. Seventy-four percent stated that the reason burglars most frequently targeted homes in which no one was home was that they feared being shot by the residence's inhabitants.

There is further evidence to support this contention. After a series of brutal rapes in Orlando, Florida, over 3,000 women were trained and outfitted with handguns. The endeavor was highly publicized. Following the training period, the total number of rapes committed dropped 90 percent. There was also a 25 percent decrease in assault and burglary in the same area.[4]

Professor Gary Kleck, a criminologist from Florida State University who researched the effects of an armed citizenry on criminal behavior, found that when victims use guns to resist crime, frequently the criminal act was disrupted and the assailant fled, leaving his would-be victim uninjured. Dr. Kleck's research also demonstrated that victims who used guns to resist robbers were less likely to lose their property than those who used another means of resistance or did nothing.

Those against gun control have also compared stringent weapons restrictions to Prohibition during the 1920s, when the possession, sale, or transportation of alcoholic beverages was outlawed. They stress that regardless of the good intentions behind such actions, it is impossible to legislate morality or erode basic personal rights that Americans have exercised since the nation's birth. They remind us that prohibiting alcoholic beverages ushered in an era of bathtub gin, speakeasies, and rumrunners. To one degree or another, formerly law-abiding citizens suddenly became involved in criminal activities, simply by having a drink or looking the other way when their neighbors did.

During Prohibition, alcohol was largely available in two forms. There were homemade brews and expensive foreign liquor, such as Scotch and whiskey, which had been smuggled into the country. Without intending to, the restrictions on alcohol helped pave the way for the rise of the vast smuggling empires operated by organized crime. Before long, law enforcement officials were left to face a national crime wave of epidemic proportions.

Opponents of gun control feel that arms restrictions might have a similar effect on our country. Approximately 70 million Americans own guns, and 25 million annually purchase hunting licenses. Some gun enthusiasts believe that these gun owners would be as willing to give up their guns as their grandfathers were to toss out their whiskey glasses.

Gun enthusiasts therefore fear that restrictive gun laws would similarly invite the creation of a criminally run black-market weapons trade. Illegal profiteers anxious for a quick return on their money might undertake large-scale gun-smuggling operations. Quality handguns purchased at low cost in Europe might command hefty sums when later sold illegally in the United States.

Gun enthusiasts fear that an ironic effect of antigun laws would be to create a new, lucrative market for organized crime. Law enforcement agencies already short of personnel in fighting a drug war might be additionally burdened in attempting to curtail the endeavors of weapons-smuggling rings. Severe weapons restrictions might inadvertently serve to make smuggling rings the most viable gun source for criminals, as well as for law-abiding citizens who merely wish to own a gun for self-protection.

They stress that for some individuals living in isolated rural areas, a gun may be the only immediate source of protection from ill-intentioned intruders. Other gun owners in closer proximity to law enforcement authorities may still feel somewhat reluctant to remain unarmed in an increasingly violent society. As one gun enthusiast put it: "I'd turn in one of my guns, but not the other. No lawmaker is going to take away the only way I can protect my family. Not when it takes the cops at least 15 minutes to respond to a call. And how many burglars are going to let you use the phone anyway?"

Those against gun control have also been quick to point out that guns can be homemade in much the same illicit manner as moonshine was during Prohibition. A number of gun magazines have carried ads similar to the one shown here:

"Cap and ball rimfire guns you can build with hand tools from simple plans and instructions. Send 25¢ stamp for illustrated brochure."

The fact that producing such a gun, let alone using a weapon of this nature, would be exceptionally dangerous doesn't alter the fact that these weapons could be inexpensively produced in someone's home. Gun control legislation would have no effect on homemade weapons.

Gun control opponents firmly believe that guns don't kill people—people kill people. They feel that as long as human beings are responsible for pulling the triggers, it's unfair to blame and outlaw the hardware. These individuals stress that new gun restrictions will not curb violence. They point to the fact that there are already many state and federal gun laws that aren't being adequately enforced.

For example, during the mid-1980s Congress passed laws that mandated jail terms of 5 to 15 years for gun-related crimes. During a three-year period in the late 1980s, firearms agents presented over 6,000 such cases to prosecutors, but little progress was made in this area. Over 90 percent of these cases were either rejected or culminated in short prison terms as the result of plea bargaining.[5]

These figures underscore the gun control opponents' claims that the present rise in violence has less to do with the availability of guns than with the failure of the justice system. They feel that as the system currently exists, it neither rehabilitates perpetrators nor keeps them confined. Many gun enthusiasts have suggested that instead of banning guns, the rising violent crime trend might best be curtailed by appointing tougher prosecutors and judges, and by building more prisons.

They stress that if a foreign army were to invade our shores, Congress would immediately appropriate adequate funds for our nation's defense. These individuals feel that a somewhat comparable situation has arisen as drug dealing criminals have initiated a domestic conflict throughout urban America. Gun control opponents believe that our nation's answer lies in removing the criminals from the streets rather than in taking guns from American homes.

President George Bush appeared to reiterate much of this sentiment when, in February of 1989, he stated: "I would strongly go after the criminals who use these guns.... The states have a lot of laws on these things. Let them enforce them."[6] The President's anticrime plan seemed to reflect these ideals as well. Although George Bush approved a ban on the import of foreign assault weapons, the President's $1.2 billion anticrime package rejected the notion of banning American-made assault rifles. Instead, his plan concentrated heavily on curtailing criminal activity. The various provisions of the plan are as follows:

• The present five-year minimum federal sentence for using a semiautomatic firearm in the commission of a crime would be doubled to a ten-year minimum. President Bush stressed that in such instances there would be "no probation, no parole." The President's anticrime package would also restrict plea bargaining and create new capital offenses for gun-related crimes.

• Bush's plan would increase both law enforcement personnel and prosecution forces. Over 825 additional federal agents and other staff members would join the ranks of the Bureau of Alcohol, Tobacco, and Firearms. Personnel in the U.S. Marshals Service and the FBI would also be supplemented. Sixteen hundred new positions would be added to the U.S. Attorney's office to assist in stepping up prosecutions.

• Among other measures, the President's plan proposes spending an additional $1 billion for new prison construction.

Many gun control opponents favored the President's anticrime program because it did not include any severe limitations on firearms. The ban on imported rifles would not significantly limit the availability of these weapons because domestic rifles, which were unaffected, effectively met the market demand. In addition, since the import ban was initiated in 1989, some U.S. manufacturers have aggressively increased their production of these guns. Yet some hard-line antigun control factions were against banning the importation of any gun, and to some degree believed that the President had betrayed their cause by doing so.

Perhaps the most powerful progun voice in America today is that of the National Rifle Association (NRA). This organization, comprised largely of hunters, sportsmen, and gun owners, stands firm in its belief that Americans have a constitutional right to own arms as guaranteed by the Second Amendment. The NRA's President is Joe Foss, a former governor of South Dakota and a highly decorated World War II hero. He described the group's convictions this way: "I say all guns are good guns. There are no bad guns. I say the whole nation should be armed. Period."[7]

Although some charge that the NRA's somewhat unyielding position against all types of gun control legislation has made it less influential in recent years, the organization nevertheless remains a potent force in the battle for the right of Americans to own firearms. The organization is made up of both men and women, although the majority of its members tend to be white, suburban, well-educated males.

Its dues-paying roster includes such celebrities as the film star Charlton Heston and the writer Michael Korda. The NRA can also boast of a vast number of highly influential political figures who have been members. These include George Bush and such past presidents as Theodore Roosevelt, Dwight Eisenhower, Richard Nixon, and Ronald Reagan. It may seem ironic that former President John F. Kennedy, who was killed by an assassin's bullet, was also an NRA member at the time of his death.

The NRA has an extensive history in the United States. It was started in 1871 by a group of former Union soldiers who were appalled by the apparent lack of shooting skills demonstrated by Northern army men during the Civil War. At that time, the newly founded organization largely centered its efforts on marksmanship and gun safety instruction.

For a number of years, the NRA largely remained an organization of hunters, gun collectors, and sports shooters. However, by the mid-1970s, the group turned some of its energy toward ensuring that the right of law-abiding Americans to own guns would not be eroded through governmental action. It established a political action committee as well as the Institute for Legislative Action to lobby for the interests of the organization's members. A membership recruitment drive was sponsored, and within the following decade membership tripled.

Throughout the years, the NRA had spent much of its funds on offering hunter safety programs, firearms instruction for police and other law enforcement personnel, and training for U.S. shooting teams involved in international Olympic competitions. In 1989 alone, over 26,000 certified NRA instructors trained 750,000 students in shooting-sports safety. In addition, 9,818 NRA certified law enforcement instructors worked on marksmanship skills development with peace officers throughout America.

Feeling that the right to keep and bear arms might be threatened by proposed gun control legislation, the NRA has shifted a good deal of its attention and annual budget toward blocking such bills. Some NRA members believe that even the mildest effort to regulate firearms would just be the beginning of a "salami game" in which the rights of American gun owners would be cut away a slice at a time. As Jim Reinke, a past NRA president, described the feeling: "If we give in on the handgun waiting period and assault rifles, we'd lose half our membership, and six months later the antigunners will want our long guns."[8]

Many opponents of gun control legislation feel that in light of the rising crime trend, a law-abiding citizen's access to arms is crucial. They frequently point to the fact that even individuals in favor of gun bans, such as *The New York Times* publisher Arthur Sulzberger and former San Francisco mayor Dianne Feinstein, have at one time obtained permits to carry concealed weapons on the basis of their public prominence.

Although it's undeniable that in some instances being armed has saved a potential victim's life, frequently the circumstances surrounding a shooting incident are not clearcut. That's what happened in the famous New York City subway shooting case involving a slim, somewhat shy 39-year-old electronics expert named Bernhard Goetz.

According to Goetz's story, he was riding a New York City subway car in December of 1984 when he was accosted by four black youths armed with sharpened screwdrivers. The young men surrounded Goetz and asked him for five dollars. Believing that they were about to beat and rob him, Goetz pulled out a handgun and fired, wounding each of them. Following the shootings, Goetz slipped away unnoticed and fled to Concord, New Hampshire. Nine days later, he turned himself in to police there.

Goetz was returned to New York to stand trial for the subway shootings. Quite a bit of furor surrounded the case. The incident received a good deal of publicity, and Goetz

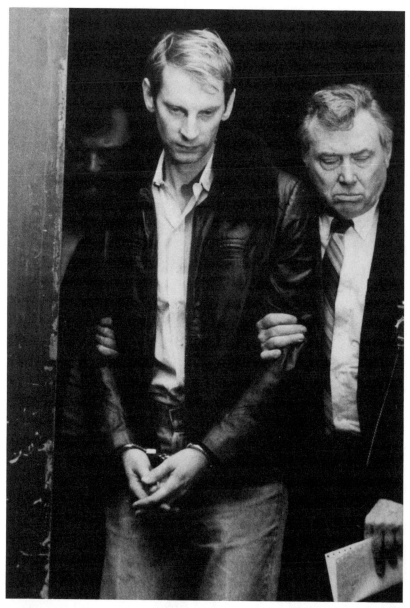

Bernhard Goetz, in handcuffs, was charged with shooting four teenagers who asked him for money on a New York City subway. The 1984 case involved heated discussion of the gun control issue.

emerged as a sort of folk hero to millions of Americans who were tired of being victims and felt it was time to fight back. In fact, at one point during his trial, Goetz received a horseshoe-shaped floral wreath from supporters in the courtroom crowd.

The public was also anxious to learn about the four men who were shot by Bernhard Goetz. Among them was Barry Allen, who at the time of Goetz's trial was in jail for chain snatching while on probation for another offense. Another victim was James Ramseur, also imprisoned when Goetz was tried, for robbing and raping a pregnant woman. Troy Canty, a third victim, testified that following his recovery from the Goetz shooting, he'd stolen money from a video game. The last victim was 19-year-old Darrel Cabey who, as a result of his encounter with Goetz, had suffered paralysis and some brain damage. He later sued Goetz in civil court for $50 million in damages. Prior to ever meeting Bernhard Goetz, Cabey had been indicted for armed robbery.

While on the witness stand at Goetz's trial, Troy Canty openly acknowledged that he'd offered three different versions of the day's events. Rather than testify, Barry Allen took the Fifth Amendment because the prosecution refused to guarantee him immunity from possible robbery charges. Darrel Cabey could not testify due to his medical condition.

James Ramseur had refused to testify initially, but after being threatened with a contempt citation, he agreed to take the stand. Unfortunately for him, Ramseur became incensed during questioning and spewed obscenities at the judge and others in the courtroom. At one point, observers in the court feared Ramseur might become violent. He took off his shoe and had to be restrained from throwing it at Goetz's attorney.

The victims' testimony, or the lack of it, made it especially difficult for the jurors to determine what had actually transpired on the subway that day. Certainly, the shooting victims had not presented a very favorable impression. However, there was also evidence that in actuality, Bernhard Goetz might be less than an all-American symbolic hero for crime-weary innocent victims.

The prosecution painted a portrait of Bernhard Goetz as a "subway vigilante" who'd been somewhat of a human volcano just waiting to erupt. Especially damaging were a number of Goetz's statements in the form of videotaped confessions to New Hampshire police following his surrender. Although Goetz never took the witness stand during his own trial, he'd been taped saying: "Look, if I had had more bullets, I would have shot 'em again and again. And I was gonna. I was gonna gouge one of the guy's eyes out with my keys afterward."[9]

Yet throughout the trial, Goetz's lawyer attempted to convince the jury that his client was the *real* victim, while the shooting "victims" were the criminals. He pointed to the fact that the 1984 subway incident was not the first time Goetz had been mugged. In 1981 Bernhard Goetz had been viciously attacked and beaten by three men. Just one of the assailants had been apprehended and had served only six months in jail. On another occasion prior to the subway shooting, Goetz was threatened by a drug addict but escaped injury. His lawyer stressed that after he'd been accosted a second time, Goetz finally resorted to carrying a gun.

According to New York law, individuals are permitted to defend themselves with deadly force if they reasonably believe that they are about to be attacked or robbed. The judge in the Goetz case had instructed the jurors to take the defendant's past experiences and state of mind into consideration in their deliberations. The jury had to decide if Goetz, who'd been previously mugged twice and had sustained serious bodily injury during one of the attacks, had acted reasonably under the circumstances.

The prosecutor argued that a reasonable person would have tried more diligently to avoid a confrontation to begin with. He suggested that Goetz might have chosen another seat on the subway further away from the four youths. He also thought that Goetz might have at least shown the gun before firing it. However, the prosecution was unable to convince the jury. Six of the 12 jurors deciding the case had at one time or another been victims of street crime. All had ridden New York City subways and were aware of the crime-infested atmosphere that can sometimes permeate these underground passageways.

Unanimously deciding that Goetz's actions were justified, the jury acquitted him for the shootings and convicted him only on the minor charge of illegal possession of a firearm. As juror Eileen Dudley, a black secretary, expressed her feelings: "I can understand what Goetz did. I was held up once. You would do anything in that situation."[10]

However, much of the black community stood divided on the Goetz issue, since the case was frequently cited as having serious racial overtones. A number of black leaders strongly denounced Goetz's acquittal, insisting that the jury had passed down a racist verdict to condone a racist act. Some charged that the trial's outcome had, in effect, declared open season on young black males.

There didn't seem to be any clear-cut answers. The case of the People vs. Bernhard Goetz had raised emotional questions about an individual's right to defend himself, juxtaposed against the inherent danger of overreacting to a situation out of irrational racist fears. The issue was debated throughout the country as well as internationally, as the Paris newspaper *Le Monde* printed: "Despite the virtuous denials of the jury, no one believed, of course, that the verdict would have been the same if the accused had been black and the victims white." Although many shared this opinion, others stressed that the Goetz case had crossed both color and class lines and had evolved into being more an instance of criminal versus victim. As evidence of this, some pointed to the case of Austin Weeks.

In 1980 Austin Weeks, a 29-year-old black man, was riding a subway in Brooklyn, New York, when he was menacingly approached by two 17-year-old white youths. One of the teenagers, Terry Zilimbinaks, bent over Weeks's seat and uttered a number of racial insults. In response, Weeks pulled an unlicensed pistol from his coat and shot Zilimbinaks, who died as a result of the injury.

As had Bernhard Goetz, Weeks quickly fled the crime scene. Although he never turned himself in, police following a number of different leads managed to track him down. Austin Weeks never stood trial, because a grand jury refused to indict him.

Although the debate over whether the lethal action taken by individuals such as Goetz and Weeks was justified may never be resolved, they nevertheless remain as examples of individuals who relied on guns to defend themselves when they perceived their lives as being threatened. They are representative of millions of Americans who will not hesitate to use their guns in the belief that victims can strike back and win. As one sign carried by a Goetz supporter outside the courtroom read: "CRIMINALS THINK TWICE OR WE WILL GOETZ YOU!"

1. *The New York Times*, April 21, 1989, p. 20.
2. ABC News Special, "Guns," January 24, 1990.
3. *Field & Stream*, April 1986, p. 37.
4. *U.S. News & World Report*, May 8, 1989, p. 28.
5. *U.S. News & World Report*, May 22, 1989, p. 10.
6. *Time*, February 27, 1989, p. 22.
7,8. *Time*, January 29, 1990, p. 6.
9. *Newsweek*, June 29, 1987, p. 22.
10. *Time*, June 29, 1987, p. 11.

THE CASE FOR
GUN CONTROL

Tony Borden (not real name), age 23, and 19-year-old Larry Borden of Maine were brothers who loved all sorts of sports and outdoor activities. They also enjoyed stylish cars, rock music, and the special game-hunting expeditions they'd undertake together, as well as with their friends.

One day the brothers bought a new .44 caliber revolver, which they were anxious to try out. They'd invited two of their friends to their home, and the four young men spent the afternoon involved in target practice in the Borden's backyard. When they'd finished, the boys sat around the kitchen table talking and laughing. Tony, who thought the pistol had been emptied because of the shots fired by the others, jokingly pointed a gun at his younger brother and pulled the trigger.

Less than a second later, the unthinkable happened. As it turned out, the gun was still loaded. The three young men watched in horror as the bullet lodged itself in Larry's chest. Terrified over what had occurred, the brothers' two friends quickly left the accident scene.

In an attempt to save his younger brother's life, Tony raced to the telephone to call for help. However, even before an ambulance and the police arrived, he realized that it was too late. Tony had accidently killed his younger brother—the person with whom he'd shared years of wonderful experiences as they'd grown up together. The pain of that reality was more than Tony Borden was able to bear. He picked up the pistol he had killed Larry with, walked out into the backyard, and shot himself in the head. Tony died immediately. The Borden family was left to mourn the loss of two sons—young men on the verge of beginning their lives, who instead died on a sunny afternoon after an hour of target shooting.

Shooting deaths involving young people cut across class, race, and geographic lines. The Borden tragedy in Maine was unfortunately indicative of thousands of similar incidents. Many of the young people killed by firearms are even younger than the Borden brothers. According to the Committee on Trauma of the American Academy of Pediatrics, gunshot wounds to children under 16 years of age in major urban areas had increased 300 percent by the late 1980s. One out of every 25 children admitted to American pediatric centers was there as the result of a gunshot wound.

The vast majority of gun-related deaths among young people occurred while children played with guns they'd found in their homes. Contributing factors to the problem included the ease of accessibility to weapons, the similarity between guns and many war toys, and the frequency of gun malfunctions. For example, within just one 6-year period, 88 California children between infancy and 14 years of age were either accidently killed by other children playing with guns or because they were playing with guns themselves.[1]

Urban black communities have been most severely affected by this phenomenon. According to the U.S. Department of Health and Human Services, the most common cause of death among black American males between 15 and 19 years of age is homicide involving the use of a gun.

One such tragic incident took place in New York City in December of 1989, when 19-year-old Arnulfo Williams, Jr., drove his 15-year-old brother Johnny to a school bus stop and decided to wait with him until the bus arrived. It seems that the younger, more slightly built boy had been beaten up at school the previous day. When Johnny had gone to his locker to put away his books, he'd found three boys there waiting for him. One boy spun Johnny around, pinning him against the wall. Then another began hitting the 15-year-old. By the time it was over, stitches were needed to close the gash left beneath his lip.

Following the assault, there were rumors that the boys weren't through with Johnny Williams yet. So Arnulfo arranged to arrive at his job a bit later that morning in order to accompany his younger brother to the bus stop. As the boys' mother, Carlotta Williams, put it: "It was just a case of big guys beating up little guys. They [her sons] decided they wanted to handle it themselves. They felt loyalty between each other. Arnulfo felt he was going to defend Johnny and stop what was taking place."[2]

The Williams brothers arrived at the bus stop to find the same three youths already there. The bullies immediately began to taunt and insult Johnny. When Arnulfo tried to break up the argument, one of the three young men took a .25 caliber semiautomatic pistol from his jacket and began shooting.

Arnulfo Williams, Jr., took one bullet in the left side of his chest. As he fell to his knees, his assailant turned to his next

target—Johnny. The 15-year-old was hit twice. The first bullet entered his left shoulder, the next struck his left leg. As the wounded brothers lay bleeding profusely in the street, the three boys quickly scattered. Johnny survived the gunshot wounds, but Arnulfo was pronounced dead on arrival at the hospital.

Perhaps Lieutenant Eugene Dunbar of the 103rd Precinct, who investigated the incident, best captured the essence of what had occurred when he said: "[It] had to be something trival between the kids that escalated. Except that one of the kids was carrying a gun."[3]

Throughout the country, individuals in favor of gun control have advocated more stringent restrictions on the use and availability of firearms. There are a number of gun control organizations in the United States that have actively co'
ducted public awareness campaigns and lobbied legislat'
to have those restraints instituted. Those in favor of
control strongly disagree with the NRA's view that /
cans have a constitutional right to bear and kee'
Morally arguing that an individual's rights end w'
infringe on the rights and welfare of others, they st'
drafting the Second Amendment, the nation's fou'
never envisioned drug gang shoot-outs or junic
students having to step through metal detec'
keep lethal weapons out of their classroom

In any case, gun control advocates point
precise wording of the Second Amen'
mention of a "citizen's right to bear arm'
of a state militia. The Amendmer'
challenged before the Supreme Cou'
who had been charged with tran'
arms across state lines defended
the Second Amendment.

Demonstrato

rs protesting hand guns in Washington, D.C.

Those in favor of gun control have emphasized that the justices were unanimous in their ruling against the men. According to Justice James C. McReynold's explanation of the Court's decision, the Second Amendment does not guarantee private citizens the right to maintain and bear guns if the weapons don't have "some reasonable relationship to the preservation or efficiency of a well regulated militia." The opinion was again underscored in 1971, when Supreme Court Justice William O. Douglas wrote that "gun purchases are not constitutional rights defended by the Second Amendment."[4]

Gun control advocates also stress that a number of eminent constitutional scholars have interpreted the Second Amendment's sole intent as that of providing a well-armed population for the purpose of national defense. They've argued that it was never meant to be tailored to the whims of individual gun owners. As Virginia attorney Stephen P. Halbrook, an authority on the Second Amendment, described its purpose: "The idea of the Founding Fathers was that tyranny would be avoided if the populace was armed."[5]

Gun control groups have expended a good deal of time, money, and effort to inform the public of political actions and decisions involving the use and abuse of weaponry. One such Washington, D.C.-based group is the Coalition to Stop Gun Violence, a national coalition of 34 religious, professional, and civic organizations with the common goal of banning the future sale of handguns to private citizens. The Coalition is also against other types of especially lethal weapons, arguing that the sale of any firearm that poses an unreasonable risk to public safety should be prohibited. According to the organization: "If the sporting and law enforcement purposes of a firearm are outweighed by the dangers of widespread private ownership of that gun, then that class of gun should be banned. Machine guns, assault weapons, Saturday Night

Specials, cop-killer bullets, and non-detectable plastic handguns all fail such a safety standard....Reducing the level of gun violence and saving lives has always been our goal."

There is a good deal of available evidence to support the view of gun control advocates that gun deaths have become nearly epidemic over the last three decades and continue to rise. For example, from 1963 to 1973, 46,121 Americans were killed in the Vietnam War. During that same period, 84,644 Americans died from gun-inflicted wounds in their homeland.[6]

Proponents of gun control also point to the fact that the United States has the highest murder rate in the world. The rate of homicidal gun deaths is over 100 times higher than in England or Wales, where gun controls are firmly in place. The likelihood of being murdered in the United States is also 200 times greater than it is in Japan—a nation in which it is extremely difficult for a private citizen to secure a gun.[7]

Handgun Control, another Washington, D.C.-based lobbying group "working to keep handguns out of the wrong hands" made available these statistics on the numbers of people killed by handguns in various countries during a one-year period.

8 people	in Great Britain
31	in Switzerland
18	in Israel
5	in Australia
8,092	in the United States

The variation in the risk factors involved in being murdered with a handgun in different countries was recently examined by researchers from both the University of Washington and the University of Tennessee. These scientists compared the number of handgun murders committed in the cities of Seattle, Washington, and Vancouver, British Columbia. The sites selected for the study were thought to be nearly ideal because the two cities were very much alike. The geography, economy, and cultural characteristics of both vicinities shared many similarities.

However, the gun control regulations in the two cities were vastly different. In Seattle, it is legal to purchase a handgun for purposes of self-defense or to get a permit to carry a concealed weapon. Only a 30-day waiting period is required. Yet just a short distance away, in Vancouver, it is illegal both to buy a handgun for self-defense or to carry a concealed weapon. Scientists hoped to see whether the stringent Canadian restrictions on handguns, passed in recent years, had in any way influenced the incidence of murder and assault in Vancouver.

The research results proved to be interesting. It was found that both cities retained nearly identical rates of robbery and burglary. The report also indicated that the number of assaults involving weapons other than guns was extremely similar as well. However, being assaulted with a gun was eight times more likely to happen in Seattle than in Vancouver.[8]

Similar variations in gun homicide rates were also shown to exist in different parts of the United States where state regulations on firearms sales differed greatly. The highest overall murder rate exists in the South, which tends to also have the highest rate of handgun ownership. Thirteen people of every 100,000 living in the South are murdered with handguns each year. This is in sharp contrast to handgun murder rates in the Northeast and North Central states, where stricter regulations on handgun ownership exist. In these regions, the annual rate of handgun deaths was only eight people per 100,000.[9] Following an examination of these comparative statistics, the U.S. General Accounting Office determined that "The ease with which firearms are obtained is a contributing factor in firearms crime."[10]

Gun control advocates stress that although gun owners often claim they need their weapons either for protection or for sporting purposes, frequently these guns are tragically misused. Dr. Arthur Kellerman of the University of Tennessee conducted an extensive study of deaths involving guns. His research, published in the *New England Journal of Medicine*, revealed that for every gun-inflicted death occurring in self-defense, there were 43 other gun deaths that had been classified as suicides, homicides, or accidental shootings. According to Dr. Kellerman, his research conclusions "shake the belief that if you have a gun in the house you are protecting yourself."[11]

His findings are echoed by the Coalition to Stop Gun Violence, which reports that 22,000 people die annually from gun-inflicted injuries—9,000 are murdered with handguns, 12,000 are the victims of handgun suicides, and 1,000 die every year from injuries resulting from shooting accidents. Sixty percent of those murdered with guns knew their killers.

Having a loaded gun handy during a heated family argument can often result in tragedy. During volatile, rage-filled moments, family members, friends, and acquaintances have been shot to death. Proponents of gun control stress that if a gun hadn't been available, the confrontation might have resulted in a bruised face or a bloodied nose rather than a funeral.

The Centers for Disease Control have revealed that in the vast majority of cases in which an individual shoots and kills a relative or friend, it is most often an unplanned, impulsive act carried out with the assistance of a loaded gun that had initially been left accessible for purposes of self-protection. In more than half of these incidents, the shooters claimed they they hadn't intended to pull the trigger when they first picked up the weapon.

As Judge Rolleen McIlwrath of the San Joaquin Municipal Court of California remarked of those who come before her in court charged with a murder that resulted from a domestic quarrel: "Even the defendants themselves ultimately, at the conclusion of the case, have said, you know, 'I didn't mean to—if the gun weren't there, I wouldn't have done it' or 'I didn't mean to shoot her. I just wish the gun hadn't been there.' Guns are so accessible, they kind of speed up the process. I'm not saying that people wouldn't ultimately, through their relationships, want to kill the other person, but they can certainly do it a lot faster with a gun."[12]

In recent years, social psychologists have also identified a fairly new phenomenon known as "weapons effect." Its essence is that the greater the exposure to weapons (firearms) the more likely angry individuals will be to use them. According to Dr. Leonard Berkowitz, a leading researcher in this field: "Sometimes [people] react mindlessly and impulsively to the presence of guns. The more control the law exercises over the availability of guns, the better."[13]

There's evidence to suggest that the rate of gun-related accidents also tends to increase with the availability of weapons. Although the circumstances surrounding these events may vary, the ultimate deadly results are the same. Women have even shot and killed their own husbands or teenage children during the late hours of the night because they'd mistaken them for burglars. Yet in other situations, gun control advocates believe that owning a gun may be detrimental for precisely the opposite reasons. They argue that having a gun can give people a false sense of security. If someone has purchased a weapon without having come to terms with whether or not he'd actually be able to take the life of another, the consequences may prove to be even deadlier than had been anticipated. It's been statistically shown that if an armed individual doesn't fire when an assailant shoots at him, it is actually more dangerous to own a weapon then to be unarmed. As *The Washington Post* quoted a police chief:

"I've worked with highly skilled and trained police officers who have failed to use deadly force when it was more than justified and appropriate. People tend to hesitate, even freeze up, in a life-threatening traumatic situation. When an attacker sees a victim lift and aim a handgun, he is hardly going to wait and see whether there is any hesitation about using it—he will most assuredly use his own weapon quickly. The police experience is that the consequences of such confrontations are often more serious than if the victim had no weapon."[14]

Often individuals who purchase firearms for self-defense are unaware of the serious emotional trauma that may result from killing another human being. It may be significant to note that over 70 percent of the police officers forced to kill someone in the line of duty leave the force within a five-year period following the shooting. Their resignations are often the result of emotional problems related to the incident.[15]

In addition, studies of police work indicate that during confrontations involving firearms, the weapon may fall into the wrong hands. During 1986, 15 police officers, who tended to be younger, stronger, and better trained in the use of weapons than their assailants, were disarmed and then either wounded or killed with their own guns. Over 85 percent of the officers who lose their weapons in confrontations with assailants are shot with their own guns.[16]

Gun control advocates feel that if police, who are professionally trained to handle such conflicts, experience these difficulties, then private citizens in similar confrontations may unexpectedly find themselves at a distinct disadvantage when facing a burglar who's just broken into their home. Proponents of gun control also emphasize that although many gun owners are law-abiding citizens, criminals have frequently stolen guns from the homes they've burglarized and later either used or sold these weapons for criminal purposes.

Accidental gun injuries and deaths span a broad range of circumstances. Gun control advocates have pointed out that although hunting is commonly considered a legitimate firearms use, too rarely do we hear about the abundance of hunting accidents that occur in the United States. The number of these incidents may seem staggering. For example, in 1989 alone, 175 people were killed—a number seven times higher than that of the American soldiers who lost their lives during the invasion of Panama that same year. In addition to the deaths, over 1,700 individuals were either injured or maimed in hunting accidents.[17]

Often these incidents occur as a result of hunters pursuing their sport in wooded areas where families as well as wildlife live. Some gun control advocates feel that since it's no longer the sixteenth century, hunting has become somewhat of an anachronism. They believe that it isn't necessary to endanger lives by hunting for food that could be safely purchased in supermarkets. They've also pointed out that there are no mandatory requirements that hunters undergo eye examinations or carry insurance. In addition, they stress that the tendency toward shooting mishaps is greatly aggravated by the fact that many hunters may drink a fair amount of beer while pursuing their sport. Beer cans have even been found among bushes, as the hunter creates a trail by which to find his way back to his camp or vehicle.

Among the most horrendous hunting deaths was that of Karen Ann Wood, a young mother of twins who lived with her family in a wooded area a few miles west of Bangor, Maine. At the time of her death, Karen was in her own backyard. She was suddenly struck in the chest by two bullets.

Karen was killed because she'd been mistaken for a deer. The fact that she had brown hair and was wearing white mittens ironically might have been a factor in why her life was taken. The hunter charged with Karen's death said that he'd seen two white-tailed deer through the trees. It's likely that the deer tails the hunter thought he saw were actually the young woman's mittens. The hunter might have been sure that he'd bring home a deer that day, but when he walked over

Rural inhabitants are often the victims of careless gun use by hunters.

to examine his kill, he found only the crumpled body of the slain woman.

Dr. Lois Howard, who was seriously wounded by a hunter, knows the horror of being mistaken for an animal and hunted down. Dr. Howard owns a home situated on 11 wooded acres in Connecticut, along the Housatonic River. Her home is actually only about a mile from the center of town.

The incident took place on a November day when Lois Howard had been out on her property posting a "NO HUNTING" sign. She described what took place:

"On the way back I was working on a trail, which I had had a boy help me clear, and I was throwing some bush over the hill and I felt this enormous heat and I saw colors that were red and yellow. I thought, 'This is November. It isn't October.' Then I heard the shot and I realized after I heard the shot—I had the sensation before I heard the report."[18]

Dr. Howard saw the man who shot her. She called out to him to help her, but instead he just stared at her and then ran in the opposite direction. Lois Howard managed to crawl back into her house to telephone for help. By the time she finally arrived at the hospital, she'd already lost 70 percent of her body's blood. Amazingly, she survived.

Gun control proponents have underscored the nightmarish quality of many of these hunting accidents. At times, bullet holes have been found in the walls, chimneys, and doors of surburban homes. Household pets and livestock have been killed while on their owners' property, because they'd been mistaken for deer. Then there's the horrifying incident of a two-year-old boy who was struck in the head by a hunter's bullet as he looked out of the window in his parents' home. After the bullet passed through the toddler, it continued through two quarter-inch pieces of plywood, struck the family's microwave oven, and eventually landed beneath the

kitchen table. Gun control advocates stress that at the very
least, hunting should be restricted in populated areas, and
they remind us that the days of Daniel Boone are over.

Still another reason why gun control proponents don't
believe that guns belong in the hands of private citizens is
that too often these weapons have been used as suicide
instruments. For the past 30 years, suicides have accounted
for over half of the nation's annual gun deaths. In fact, the
United States has the dubious distinction of having the
world's highest rate of gun-related suicides. In 1986 (the latest
year for which complete statistics are available) 7.5 people
out of every 100,000 used guns to kill themselves. At 6 percent,
Switzerland had the second highest rate, while in France the
rate of gun-inflicted suicides was 4.9 percent, followed by
Canada at 4.7 percent.[19]

A survey conducted by *Time* magazine revealed that in
recent years, a growing number of young people have begun
to use guns to kill themselves. Some young men have shot
themselves after being abandoned by their girlfriends. Young
women have also pointed a gun to their heads and pulled the
trigger, dying in their boyfriends' presence.

Suicide is the third leading cause of death among adoles-
cents. By the late 1980s, suicides among children between 10
and 14 years of age had doubled. Over half of these deaths
were gun inflicted.[20]

Proponents of gun control underscore the finality guns
lend to suicide attempts. Guns are generally considered the
most deadly means of suicide. The overwhelming majority of
suicide attempts involving guns are successful. It's been
frequently pointed out by psychotherapists that many people
who attempt suicide don't really wish to die. Often the
gesture is merely a disguised call for help. Some therapists
believe that for each suicide resulting in death, there may be

as many as 20 attempts from which individuals are successfully rescued. Many physicians feel that suicide attempts often result from depression that may be treatable with drugs, psychotherapy, or a combination of both.

Less lethal means of suicide such as breathing in carbon monoxide from a car exhaust, overdosing on pills, or swimming too far from the shore afford a possible opportunity for rescue. However, there's a scant possibility of survival if someone places a gun in his mouth and pulls the trigger.

One such incident involved the death of a 66-year-old widow from Georgia. Although the woman had been left ample funds by her deceased husband, she was continually haunted by a fear of abject poverty, which she believed might entail living out the remainder of her days on the city streets as a homeless person.

She had tried to end her life twice with an overdose of pills, but fortunately in both instances she was found in time and saved. Finally, she began treatment for her recurring bouts of severe depression. At first, she appeared to be making good progress, but then she experienced a setback. Depressed one day, she walked into a gun dealer's shop at a nearby shopping mall. The woman, who knew nothing about weapons, had never even held a gun. Unfortunately, the clerk who sold her one proved to be all too helpful. At the woman's request, he even loaded the weapon for her.

The woman took the gun home and later that day, while still feeling depressed, used it to kill herself. This time, there was nothing anyone could do to help her. There wasn't an opportunity to pump her stomach to dissolve the effects of a potentially lethal pill overdose. Now the results were irrevocable. She'd blown her head away.

Therapists later suggested that the right medication might eventually have been found for her, and the woman's depression might have been successfully treated. They believe she might have felt much differently about her life and that suicide would not even have been an option. Gun control advocates stress that now she'd never have the chance to know. A gun had made her decision final.

Is a woman whose judgment was clouded by a serious mental disorder at the time of the shooting solely responsible for her subsequent death? The Legal Action Project of the gun control group known as The Center to Prevent Handgun Violence recently began a nationwide initiative to more closely examine cause and liability in such instances.

For example, in late March of 1981, an assistant manager named Olen Kelley was shot during a store robbery. The gun that lodged a bullet in Mr. Kelley's chest is known as a "Saturday Night Special." This small, easy-to-conceal, cheaply made weapon is frequently used for criminal purposes. The gun's short barrel and poor quality limit its use to close-range shots. It's an inefficient weapon for self-defense or sporting purposes.

Since the gun is most effective only within a criminal context, Mr. Kelley felt it was unreasonable for the weapon's manufacturers to be totally free of liability for repercussions caused by its product. He sued the manufacturer in a court of law and won. His case's decision resulted in a precedent-setting ruling by Maryland's Supreme Court. For the first time, weapons manufacturers were held accountable for the injury inflicted on innocent people by their products when used for criminal purposes.

The Center to Prevent Handgun Violence believes that weapons such as Saturday Night Specials or military-style assault rifles are only useful for criminal endeavors when placed in civilian hands. They feel the resulting human suffering and economic loss should not be shared solely by the innocent victims and American taxpayers. The dollars-and-cents cost of weapon-related injuries are high. A study recently published in the *Journal of the American Medical Association* indicated that taxpayers supply most of the estimated $1 billion annually spent for hospitalization and other related firearm injury costs.[21]

The Center would like to see these costs shifted to the manufacturers of such killing devices, whom they believe are ultimately responsible for these weapons falling into criminal hands. Such liability would extend to manufacturers who produce guns suitable solely for criminal activity, gun dealers who violate state mandated waiting periods in their sales' policies, individuals who sell guns to impaired persons, as well as gun owners who leave loaded weapons within the reach of children.

The goal of the Legal Action Project of the Center to Prevent Handgun Violence is to use the legal system to help remedy the tragedy of gun violence. In addition to bringing cases to court, the Project will also help victims and their families to have more of a say at the parole hearings of perpetrators whose crimes involved firearms. To achieve its aims, the project is assembling a network of private attorneys throughout the nation to assist victims of gun misuse in being effectively represented before judges and juries. Their goal in establishing important legal precedents is to ultimately reduce the accessibility of dangerous firearms for criminal purposes.

Gun control advocates hope that those responsible for the injury and deaths will consider the impact of cases such as the following:

• In 1989 a New York jury held a department store liable for selling a shotgun to an obviously intoxicated man who then used the weapon on an innocent person. The victim was permanently paralyzed as a result of the shooting. The jury awarded the injured person $2.4 million in damages.

• When a teenager suffered severe brain damage after accidently shooting himself with a pistol sold to him by a Pennsylvania gun dealer, the jury held the gun dealer responsible for not demonstrating how to properly use the weapon, as well as for not providing explicit written instructions for the weapon's use at the time of the sale. The young person was awarded $11.3 million in damages.

• In Connecticut, a school janitor died after being fatally shot with a TEC-9 assault weapon. His family sued the weapon's manufacturer for marketing the gun to civilians, since the weapon is primarily suited for criminal purposes. A study showing that the particular semiautomatic in question is most frequently used in crime had been introduced into the testimony.

Proponents of gun control refute the argument of gun enthusiasts that some degree of criminal violence may be the price of living in a society that cherishes and protects individual freedoms. As the wife of a police officer from Plantation, Florida, said:

"As the wife of one police officer who has been in one gun fight and lived, every morning I watch him put on a bulletproof vest, strap on a gun and leave, wondering if I'll have to explain to our son that Dad wasn't so lucky in the next gun fight, but that the other guy's rights were preserved."[22]

In recent years, gun control advocates have striven to restrict the availability of assault weapons, since these guns are frequently found on the front lines of crime. According to the Federal Bureau of Alcohol, Tobacco, and Firearms: "An assault gun is 20 times more likely to be used in a crime than a conventional firearm....Assault guns showed up in nearly 30 percent of all firearms traced to organized crime, gun trafficking, and crimes committed by terrorists in the United States between 1988 and 1989."

Gun control proponents have also expressed concern over the large number of American-made assault rifles currently being exported to other countries. Ironically, these weapons may be instrumental in the drug flow into this country. Colombian drug traffickers can obtain them easily, and the rifles are frequently employed as enforcement instruments in illegal drug smuggling businesses.

A special agent with the Bureau of Alcohol, Tobacco, and Firearms indicated that 87 percent of a sample of firearms confiscated from drug traffickers by the Colombian government proved to be of American origin. As DEA official David Webster stated before the House Select Committee on Narcotics Abuse and Control: "There's no question about the

U.S. Customs inspectors examine semiautomatic weapons seized at Miami International Airport as the guns were about to be shipped to Colombia, a major drug supplier. Drug dealers have increasingly turned to the use of such weapons in their battles with law enforcement groups.

escalation of heavy weaponry moving toward the cartels. Most of these weapons are coming from the United States."[23] Gun control activists point to the inherent futility of U.S. demands that Colombian officials take firmer measures against drug traffickers when, in actuality, the traffickers' most deadly enforcement tools are largely supplied by American weapons manufacturers.

Gun control groups have also spoken out against plastic guns that are capable of passing undetected through airport security systems. Plastic guns initially came to the public's attention several years ago, when it was first learned that Libyan President Muammar Kaddafi had attempted to purchase over 100 of these pistols. Gun control advocates stress that these guns could be used for criminal purposes in courtroom situations as key witnesses testify, on airplanes, or perhaps even to pass through White House Secret Service checks. In fact, the guns have sometimes even been referred to as "terrorists' specials."

As one California police chief said of the plastic pistols: "These weapons are for war and combat and have no place in urban society."[24] In addition, various gun control groups have also taken a stand against "cop-killer bullets." This Teflon-coated ammunition is designed to penetrate the bulletproof vests frequently worn by police officers on duty.

In an interview with the author, Michael Beard, executive director of the Coalition to Stop Gun Violence, expressed his feelings about arms in America as follows:

"I've been involved in gun control for a number of years now. In the beginning we were concerned about 25-year-olds with revolvers. Now we're worried about 14-year-olds in urban areas with machine guns. So far Congress has already passed some important gun control legislation. We have to continue in that direction. If this doesn't happen, we will eventually lose a generation of youths. Unfortunately, this is already happening in some urban black communities.

"Or we may step back into the good old shoot-it-out days of the Wild West. Everyone will be carrying a gun, and that's how disputes will be settled. It wouldn't be a question of who's right, but rather who's quicker on the draw. Firearms technology is becoming so advanced that it's running away with itself. It would be tragic to live in a world where people would be afraid of stepping on someone's shoes finding a seat in a movie theater for fear of being shot to death."

While some gun control advocacy groups have employed media advertisements and lobbying techniques to achieve their goals, work at a grass-roots level continues as well. One Catholic priest from Denver, Colorado, offered his parishioners an unusual option in an attempt to curb violence in the area. He paid $100 for every gun turned in to him at the church. Before the funds for this project ran out, the priest had collected 35 handguns and four shotguns.

Tired of officiating at shooting-death funerals, the priest wished to extend the project's significance by eventually collecting enough weapons to melt the guns down for a new church bell. Perhaps the enormity of the task faced by gun control proponents was best underscored when it was learned that one of the men who'd turned in a pistol to the priest was planning to use his $100 reward as a down payment on an assault rifle.

---

1. *Journal of the American Medical Association*, June 12, 1988, pp. 3107–3109.
2,3. *The New York Times*, December 2, 1989, p. 32.
4. *The New York Times*, July 26, 1989, p. A23.
5. *The New York Times*, April 2, 1989, p. 20.
6. FBI Crime Reports, Annual Crime Surveys, 1963–1973.
7. *Congressional Record*, February 22, 1983.

8. *The Washington Post,* November 8, 1988, p. A4.

9. FBI Crime Reports, 1986, p. 13.

10. General Accounting Office, "Handgun Control Effectiveness and Costs," p. 33.

11. *U.S. News & World Report,* June 23, 1986, p. 9.

12. ABC News Special, "Guns," January 24, 1990.

13. *Milwaukee Journal,* June 26, 1981, p. 31.

14–16 *The Washington Post,* November 16, 1987, p. 8.

17,18. "Geraldo," CBS-TV, January 23, 1990.

19,20. *Time,* July 17, 1989, p. 61.

21. Center to Prevent Handgun Violence Bulletin, July 1989, p. 6.

22. *U.S. News & World Report,* March 31, 1986, p. 74.

23. *The Washington Post,* November 2, 1989, p. A12.

24. *Newsweek,* June 1, 1987, p. 31.

5

SUNSHINE AND TEARS:

AN EXPERIMENT IN

LIFTING GUN

CONTROLS

By the mid 1980s, Florida residents had grown increasingly exasperated by the upsurge of violent crime in America's Sunshine State. A steady flow of drug traffic in some areas, compounded by other social problems, had put Florida legislators under pressure to find a means to contain the rampant criminal activity affecting their jurisdictions. For some months, elected representatives had discussed the pros and cons of an armed citizenry. They pondered the effects of making guns more readily available to law-abiding Floridians. Would criminals really be less likely to attack a potentially armed victim? Or might they simply use easily accessed weapons for their own illicit purposes?

Gun control opponents felt certain that lifting gun controls would improve the situation. As one member of the state rifle association put it: "If I want to mug someone, I'll avoid a person who may have a handgun."[1] Indeed, gun enthusiasts had frequently stressed that in some sections of Florida, where criminals supposedly outnumbered honest citizens 20 to 1, police had generally been ineffective in curbing crime.

Apparently, much of this sentiment was shared by Florida legislators when, in May of 1987, Florida Governor Bob Martinez signed a bill, to go into effect in October of that year, that dramatically lessened restrictions on civilian-owned weapons. In some ways, the Florida bill delivered a two-pronged victory to progun forces within the state. One portion of the bill abolished the state's 400 local gun control laws, while another provision permitted citizens to more easily carry concealed weapons. The bill also virtually eliminated waiting periods for gun purchasers.

With the bill's passage, Florida became the thirty-first state to prohibit various localities from passing their own firearms restrictions. Antigun-control forces had long argued that these often inconsistent regulations infringed on the constitutional rights of sportsmen. For example, they pointed to the case of an Olympic shooting team member who'd been arrested in the town of Treasure Island, Florida, for violating a local gun ordinance when he posed for a picture while holding his rifle.

Public reaction to the lifting of Florida gun controls was somewhat mixed. Perhaps Marion Hammer of the NRA affiliate, the United Sportsmen of Florida, spoke for a good portion of the state's population when describing the new bill's intent as that of "restoring the right of every law-abiding citizen...to keep and bear arms for lawful self-defense."[2] Many crime-weary Floridians seemed to welcome the opportunity to be armed in a state in which the narcotics industry had boomed. From 1986 to 1987 alone (the year prior to the bill's passage), violent crime in the state had increased by 12 percent.[3]

Under the new Florida law, residents only had to pay a $146 processing fee and take a required two-hour safety class on firearm use in order to be issued a concealed-weapons permit. Anyone who was 21 years of age or older, had lived in Florida for at least six months, and had no prior police record was eligible to apply for a permit. Immediately following the law's passage, more than 36,000 applications flooded state offices. More than 65 new employees had to be hired in order to process them.

However, not everyone was pleased with the changes in Florida's firearms regulations. Although gun control advocates conceded that high crime areas existed within the state, they stressed that in the year prior to the new bill's passage, over half the handgun killings in Florida had occurred between people who knew one another.

A number of Florida police officers also expressed a mixed reaction to the new law. Although they welcomed the assistance of an armed citizenry in thwarting criminal activity, some officers feared that their own safety might now be further jeopardized by stray bullets from poor shots. As Jim Lelyjedal of the Broward County sheriff's office predicted: "We foresee more accidental and unintentional shootings."[4]

Law enforcement officials also expressed concern over the prospect of possibly having to confront many more thousands of gun-bearing individuals with concealed weapons. One member of the force may have best summarized the prevailing sentiment when he cited how many officers had grown somewhat uneasy over "being unable to distinguish who is a good guy and who is a bad guy."[5] Some Florida officers were warned by their superiors to exercise extreme caution in even routine traffic stops. Since the new law voided the ten-day waiting period during which background checks were conducted, some police officers also wondered if an entirely new class of gun owner might emerge—impulse weapon buyers who wouldn't have gone through with the gun purchase if they'd been forced to wait.

Even in its infancy, however, the new Florida gun law began to undergo changes. The bill's passage had wiped out a 1893 law that prohibited individuals from openly carrying their weapons in public. Many residents now expressed their fears that the streets might soon be lined with individuals whose pistols protruded from their pockets or who wandered through town with shotguns tucked beneath their arms.

Fearing liability suits that might ensue from shooting accidents on their premises, numerous store owners posted signs that read "DON'T CARRY YOUR GUNS IN HERE." Entrepreneurs dependent on state tourism for their livelihood were upset by the negative barrage of media publicity that followed as a consequence of the new legislation. In satirical cartoons and editorials, Florida had been dubbed the "Dodge City of the South" and "America's Gunshine State." Some even comically suggested that the state's official bird ought to be the skeet.

An attempt was made to rectify the situation. Only nine days after the bill's passage, the Florida legislature voted unanimously to close what had been known as the law's "Dodge City" loophole, which permitted carrying guns in public as long as the weapon was clearly visible. As one relieved representative said of the reversal: "I think we've taken the first step toward restoring sanity to our streets."[6]

Florida residents' feelings about relaxed gun controls in their state frequently reflect their own experiences. Some have undoubtedly benefited from having been armed in fending off or even surviving a criminal attack. For example, when 28-year-old Linda Fincher saw a man she didn't know coming toward her in a Pensacola, Florida, parking lot, she assumed that he was merely a well-meaning individual who wished to assist her in moving from her wheelchair into the seat of her car.

Unfortunately, the stranger's intent was not as noble as might have been hoped. Instead, he approached Ms. Fincher, grabbed her purse, and immediately ran to another car in which a driver was ready to help him flee. Linda Fincher also hurriedly entered her vehicle, as did a bystander who happened to witness the crime. Fincher and the witness gave chase in their cars, and managed to cut off the fleeing vehicle.

At that point, Linda Fincher pulled out her revolver, aiming it directly at the car's driver. The thief, who sat in the passenger's seat, told her not to shoot and tossed the stolen purse back to her. As he hurled it, the man added, "It's all there." Although the thieves escaped, Ms. Fincher was glad to have retrieved her purse and to find that the $400 contained in it had been left untouched.

Miami, Florida, cab driver Mark Yuhr had only recently been licensed to carry a concealed weapon under the state's new liberal gun law when he was attacked by a passenger armed with a pistol. The passenger demanded money, then threatened the cab driver's life. When the robber momentarily glanced in the other direction, Yuhr reached for his own .45 and shot his assailant. As it turned out, the man who attempted to rob Mark Yuhr had an extensive criminal record. He'd been convicted for armed robbery, firearm violations, and attempted first-degree murder of a police officer. The local police said of the incident: "This sends a major message to the rest of the robbers out there."

Miami resident José Barrios was also glad he had his gun the second time armed robbers arrived at his small food market. At the time of the first robbery, Barrios didn't have a weapon. He was shot in the head, and lost his left eye as a result of the injury. The next time two armed men tried to rob him, Barrios was prepared. When the thieves demanded cash while pointing a gun at him, the store owner surprised them by drawing out his own gun and firing. After Barrios wounded one of the men, both robbers fled from the store. They were later found and arrested on armed robbery and related charges.

While these Florida residents benefited from owning a gun, others tell a very different story. One afternoon ten-year-old Sean Smith and his eight-year-old sister Erin returned to their home in Miramar, Florida, after a day at the Sunshine Elementary School. The children were home alone. As Sean looked for a Nintendo video game cassette, he came across his father's loaded .38 caliber pistol.

Sean decided to play with the gun instead of searching further for the video game. He picked up the weapon, pointed it out the window, and pulled the trigger. Sean never meant to hit anyone, but he did. The bullet struck his little sister in the chest.

Bleeding profusely, the small girl fell to the ground. Realizing what he'd done, the young boy started to cry. However, the ten-year-old still had sufficient composure to dial 911 for help. Unable to hold back his tears, Sean Smith told the operator: "I didn't know my Dad's gun was loaded and…and I shot her. Please don't die. Please, God. Please, don't be dead."[7] Moments later an emergency rescue squad arrived only to find Erin already dead.

The eight-year-old's death seemed symptomatic of a rash of accidental Florida shootings that resulted in child fatalities or injuries. On the same day Erin Smith died, a ten-year-old Florida boy was shot by his thirteen-year-old friend as the older boy showed him a gun belonging to his stepfather. The next day, only miles away, four-year-old Evie Lynn Hagan fought with her six-year-old brother over a gun the children had accidentally found in a cupboard. The gun went off, and Evie was hit. The bullet left the young girl paralyzed. Within the next few days several other accidental shootings in which young children were either killed or wounded occurred within the state.

The tragic shootings of children by other children that took place in June of 1989 shook the sensibilities of Florida residents. Increasing numbers of people became conscious of what it was like to lose a child during the "Killing Season," the summer period during which the highest number of child gun fatalities take place. Prompted by public concern, Florida governor Bob Martinez included new gun safety legislation in a special state legislative session. Although he'd initially resisted the bill the governor, along with much of the population, had been galvanized into action by the recent wave of child shootings. As Martinez explained: "If we can pass legislation that makes just one parent act more carefully, that saves just one child...our efforts will be worthwhile."[8]

The bill passed by the Florida legislature requires gun owners to take reasonable safety precautions in the handling and storage of their weapons in environments in which children under 15 years of age are present. The law defines reasonable precautions as measures such as using the trigger lock or keeping the weapon in a locked box. Provisions in the law include exemptions for accidents occurring during supervised hunting expeditions and target practice. There are also exclusions for incidents in which the gun was stolen.

According to the bill, if an adult fails to secure a loaded gun and the weapon is used by a minor in an accidental shooting, the gun owner can be charged with a felony. The maximum penalty for the offense is five years in prison and a $5,000 fine. In instances in which a minor displays a loaded gun or threatens someone with it, the gun owner may be charged with a misdemeanor. This offense carries a maximum penalty of 60 days in jail and a $500 fine.

Proponents of the bill hoped the new legislation would force parents to exercise better judgment in safeguarding their children from the consequences of playing with lethal weapons. However, progun forces argued that it was impossible to legislate common sense, and since that was the essence of the new bill, it was actually worthless. As Tracey Martin, manager of education and training for the National Rifle Association, had said: "More children die by drowning than from gunshot wounds, but do we demand that the government ban swimming pools? No, we teach water safety. It's the same with firearms—we need to teach children and adults firearm safety."[9]

Gun enthusiasts further feel that if the potential death of your own child isn't sufficient motivation to keep a gun safely locked away, then a new law would surely not make parents act more responsibly. Proponents of the law believe otherwise. They regard the law regulating gun safety as similar to the legislation requiring that seat belts be used in motor vehicles. While it might be argued that the risk of injury would be enough to ensure the wide use of seat belts, that hasn't always been the case. However, gun control advocates have pointed out that the Florida law mandating that seat belts be used both increased their usage and reduced injuries.

Yet some progun forces believe the law is really more of an attempt to enhance the state's image than a genuine means of promoting accident prevention. Many feel that prosecuting a parent who must already cope with the loss or injury of a

As part of its gun education program, the National Rifle Association (NRA) produces such materials as coloring books to teach gun safety.

child through an accidental shooting would only serve to inhumanely compound the tragedy.

The tragedy becomes especially vivid in the case of Evie Lynn Hagan, one of the young shooting victims whose injury prompted passage of the bill. According to one of the little girl's physicians: "Evie will likely be ventilator-dependent for the rest of her life, and will probably be bedridden and wheelchair bound, with little lower motor function except in her extremities."[10] Gun control opponents argue that imprisoning someone like Evie's father would probably only bring greater pain and distress to the child, as well as to other family members. Those in favor of the law hope that it will help to prevent other children from sharing Evie's fate, or worse. Only time will tell who's correct.

---

1. *U.S. News & World Report,* May 25, 1987, p. 14.

2,3,4. *U.S. News & World Report,* October 12, 1987, p. 16.

5. *The New York Times,* October 25, 1987, p. 16.

6. *Time,* October 19, 1987, p. 25.

7. *The New York Times,* June 18, 1989, p. 20.

8. *USA Today,* June 15, 1989, p. 3A.

9,10. *People Weekly,* July 10, 1989, p. 57.

LEGISLATION

The conflict over gun control in Florida is in some ways representative of the broader national picture. While gun battles have sometimes been fought out on American streets, legislative wars of seemingly comparable magnitude have also been waged over gun control on both a state and national level. The present federal legislation that provides for the national regulation of firearms is the Gun Control Act of 1968. This law prohibits criminals, minors, the mentally ill, illegal aliens, and drug addicts from legally purchasing handguns. In addition to this law, numerous states and some localities have their own gun control laws that place further restrictions on the possession and sale of firearms.

As might be expected, pro- and anti-gun control factions view the Gun Control Act of 1968 quite differently. In actuality, however, neither side is satisfied with it. The National Rifle Association is against the legislation because they feel it imposes unreasonable curbs on law-abiding citizens wishing to purchase guns. On the other hand, gun control advocates feel that the law doesn't do nearly enough to safeguard the lives of innocent people. They stress that in states in which no waiting period or background check is required, anyone with sufficient cash can enter a gun dealer's shop and leave with a weapon.

Forces on both sides of the issue have supported measures for change. In 1986 the NRA and other antigun-control groups backed the McClure-Volkner Bill (the Firearms Owners' Protection Act), which included provisions to allow mail-order gun sales and interstate rifle and shotgun sales. In addition, the legislation limited federal law enforcement agencies to only one annual unannounced inspection of a gun dealer's premises. The NRA claimed the bill was designed to prevent harassment of innocent individuals for inadvertent technical violations of the Gun Control Act of 1968. According to the NRA, testimony by the Bureau of Alcohol, Tobacco, and Firearms revealed that 75 percent of the individuals found to have violated the Gun Control Act of 1968 actually proved to be law-abiding citizens. A former spokesperson for the National Rifle Association expressed the group's sentiments:

"Persons who own firearms are not second-class citizens; we are entitled to the same civil rights as everyone else in this country. Unfortunately, this hasn't always been the case. Under the existing federal firearms law, the Gun Control Act of 1968, law-abiding gun owners—including sportsmen, competitors, licensed dealers and collectors—have been presumed guilty until proven innocent."[1]

Gun control advocates stood in opposition to the bill, claiming that the legislation would turn back the clock on the progress achieved through the Gun Control Act of 1968. Newspaper cartoonists criticized the McClure-Volkner bill as they depicted both handguns and machine guns readily available through coin-operated vending machines. There were charges that if the legislation passed, criminals as well as insane individuals would be able to order as many guns as they desired through the mail. Despite the onslaught of criticism, in the end, the NRA was victorious. The McClure-Volkner bill was passed by Congress.

There have, however, been substantial gun control victories on a national level as well. Gun control lobbying forces teamed up with large numbers of the nation's police to persuade Congress to pass a bill banning "cop killer" bullets (ammunition capable of piercing the bulletproof vests worn by police). In response to further gun control lobbying efforts, Congress also passed a bill to ban plastic handguns, which can easily pass through metal detectors.

Another piece of legislation gun control forces have ardently pressed for is the Brady Handgun Violence Prevention Act, commonly known as the Brady Bill. The bill is named for James Brady, former White House press secretary, and his wife, Sarah. James Brady, along with former President Reagan and two law enforcement officers, was shot by a man named John Hinckley, who had walked into a Dallas, Texas, pawnshop and bought a handgun. Hinckley lied on his weapons application and was able to purchase the gun easily. Because Texas state law did not require a waiting period during which a background check might be conducted, there was nothing to stop Hinckley from buying a gun and shooting the president of the United States and others surrounding him.

The proposed Brady Bill would require a seven-day waiting period when purchasing a handgun from a li-

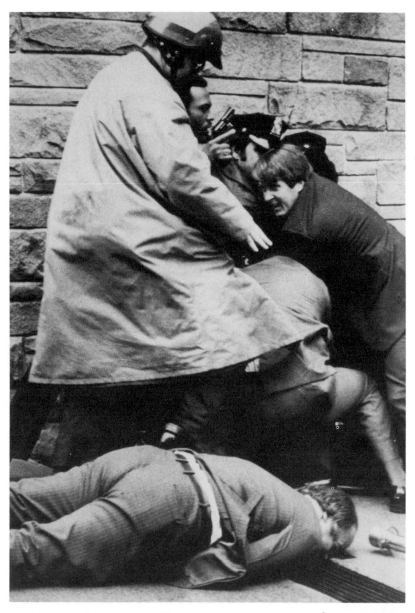

President Ronald Reagan and his press secretary, James Brady, shown here face down, were shot by a would-be assassin in 1981. The shooting resulted in increased demands for greater gun controls.

censed gun dealer. Gun control proponents stress that the bill would help reduce gun violence on two levels. The imposed week-long waiting period would afford local police ample time in which to do background checks on would-be gun purchasers. The seven-day purchase delay would also serve as a cooling-off period for someone who might buy a firearm with which to settle a heated argument, or for a clinically depressed person who might commit suicide while despondent.

Gun control proponents stress that waiting periods have been shown to be effective in reducing handgun violence. As evidence, they point to the experience of states that have passed their own waiting period legislation. For example, the superintendent of the New Jersey State Police has reported that during the 20 years in which their state law has beeen in existence, over 10,000 convicted felons have been caught attempting to purchase handguns.

According to the Maryland State Police, during 1986 alone, Maryland's newly enacted seven-day waiting period prevented 732 unqualified potential gun buyers from making these purchases. A similar trend was identified in California. California's Department of Justice indicated that over the course of a year, the state's 15-day waiting period prevented 1,515 convicted criminals from buying handguns.[2]

If the Brady Bill were passed, would-be handgun purchasers would fill out a form indicating that they are not disqualified from buying a handgun according to the criteria set forth by the Gun Control Act of 1968. The gun dealer would then forward a copy of the handgun purchase application to the local law enforcement authorities. The police would conduct the background check. If the gun dealer did not receive word within a week that the buyer wasn't qualified, he could proceed with the sale. Unless the sale had been prohibited, the law enforcement agency would be required to destroy any existing copies of the background check within a month.

If enacted, the Brady Bill would generally regulate gun sales nationwide. It would not, however, apply to states where a week-long waiting period is already in existence or where procedures for procuring background checks have already been instituted. The bill would provide for the sale of guns in less than seven days if law enforcement authorities have notified the authorized gun dealer that the applicant's eligibility had been verified. Under the Brady Bill, a dealer who knowingly violates the waiting period would be guilty of a misdemeanor.

The Brady Bill was introduced during the 100th Congress. It received a great deal of support from various sectors. On June 21, 1988, President Ronald Reagan openly endorsed having both a waiting period and a background check for those wishing to purchase handguns. Many police organizations, which in the past had frequently sided with the NRA in its opposition to gun regulations, also endorsed the Brady Bill. As indicated by the stand taken by the Fraternal Order of Police (198,000 members):

"If the seven-day waiting period will insure just one life—the life of a law enforcement officer or a citizen—then [Congress's] work will be successful. Our prediction is that a 'cooling off' period will save hundreds of lives."[3] The National Association of Police Organizations (80,000 members) and other police groups spoke out in favor of the proposed legislation as well.

However, the NRA insisted that the bill posed unfair restrictions on law-abiding gun owners and launched a heavy lobbying offensive against its passage. The Brady Bill was defeated, and the NRA's efforts have frequently been credited with its demise. In its place, progun forces pushed through a substitute amendment that they heralded as being far more effective. It is known as the McCollum Amendment.

Introduced by Republican representative Bill McCollum of Florida, the amendment provided that the Attorney General would "develop a system for the immediate and accurate identification of felons who attempt to purchase firearms." As to the type of system instituted, McCollum favored a sophisticated computerized fingerprinting system. The NRA specified that such a system would ideally be quick and easy—"just like using your VISA card."

Under the best of circumstances, implementation of the McCollum Amendment would remain uncomplicated. A potential gun purchaser would select the weapon he wished to buy from a gun dealer. While the buyer was still at the gun shop, a sales clerk would take his fingerprints. The prints would then be electronically transmitted to a national computer data bank, where they'd be scanned against a compilation of criminal prints. It would only take moments to determine if the potential purchaser's prints matched those of a convicted felon. Depending on the outcome, the individual would either be sold the weapon or sent away empty handed.

If this "immediate answer" system sounds too good to be true, gun control advocates feel that's because it is. They argue that the McCollum Amendment isn't workable because the proposed scheme is too advanced for present-day technology. When accessing fingerprints, computers can only detect similarities on a very broad basis. A highly trained eye is still necessary in the painstaking process of determining a final positive identification.

Of course, other types of systems might be devised. It's presently possible to immediately check names and addresses against those contained in a centralized data bank. However, that would mean having to procure a computer for the nearly 300,000 licensed gun dealers in the United States—a fairly expensive proposition. There would also be the problem of rooting out potential purchasers who misrepresented themselves by presenting false identification.

Some critics of the McCollum Amendment have suggested that the proposal raises important issues regarding civil liberties. They question if a computerized data bank comprised of FBI criminal files available to gun store owners across America could lead to confidentiality violations as well as to other possible abuses.

In addition, gun control proponents have still not given up on the Brady Bill. They've pointed to the fact that in the 100th Congress, the bill was only narrowly defeated— by a mere 24 votes. Since its initial defeat, the Brady Hill has been reintroduced in the 101st Congress.

Meanwhile, the NRA remains firm in its opposition to gun controls. The organization has done a great deal of lobbying on a state level to ensure that localities are prohibited from passing their own gun control laws. So far, it has been successful in 34 states and it continues to work for similar legislation in other areas.

Gun control advocates have made significant breakthroughs at the state level as well. In February 1989, the Virginia General Assembly passed a law that requires criminal background checks for prospective purchasers of pistols with barrels shorter than five inches long (Saturday Night Specials) or assault rifles with weapon clips of more than 20 rounds. Gun control lobbyists were also instrumental the previous year in helping to convince Maryland lawmakers to ban further sales of Saturday Night Specials in their state. Attempting to reverse the decision, progun forces actively campaigned to have the law repealed. However, Maryland residents voted to retain the legislation.

Within various states, some municipalities have taken stringent measures to ban weapons among its citizenry. For example, a number of Chicago suburbs such as Wilmette, Oak Park, Morton Grove, and Evanston have banned the private possession of pistols within their town borders.

In Washington, D.C., which has sometimes been unflatteringly referred to as the murder capital of the nation, the City Council passed a bill to further strengthen local gun control laws by implementing a new twist on the concept of liability. The new law classifies guns as inherently dangerous products. Therefore, both gun manufacturers and gun dealers who sell firearms may now be held financially liable for any damage incurred through their use. The City Council hopes the legislation will encourage gun dealers to try to keep weapons from falling into the wrong hands. As one City Council member said: "The statute will attempt to do through the handgun industry's pocketbooks what was not done through their consciences."[4]

Gun control proponents have also encouraged legislative proposals to outlaw assault rifles. Momentum to ban these deadly weapons in California increased following a wave of gang shootings and Patrick Purdy's tragic massacre of elementary school children.

To dramatize the destructiveness of assault rifles, members of the Los Angeles Police Force provided a televised demonstration of the weapon's lethal capabilities. Viewers were able to see firsthand how a single bullet from the gun could instantly shatter a cinder block. The day after the TV demonstration, the Los Angeles County Board of Supervisors voted 3 to 1 to urge the legislature to ban the guns.

Gun lobbyists argued that banning a particular weapon would be inherently discriminatory. They stressed that the rifles are highly valued by collectors, and sometimes used by law-abiding citizens for "plinking," or shooting tin cans. They also insisted that the actual differences between military and hunting guns are negligible. As David W. Conover, a lobbyist for the NRA, stated: "It's called an assault weapon by people who want to ban it, a rifle by those who don't. It has a romantic sound to it. But there's no technical difference between semiautomatic rifles that are assault and those that are conventional."[5]

Gun control proponents claimed that there is a difference. Although some sportsmen use semiautomatic rifles for hunting purposes, a rifle that holds 20 or more cartridges is far more characteristic of a military assault weapon than one used by legitimate sportsmen. In hunting migratory birds, federal law already limits to three the number of rounds that can be used with a shotgun. In addition, numerous states have placed various restrictions on the number of ammunition rounds hunters may use when hunting with either semiautomatic rifles or shotguns.

Gun control advocates also pointed out that none of the 50 types of semiautomatic rifles, pistols, and shotguns to be banned in California are used by hunters. The growing public sentiment was perhaps best expressed by Senator Howard M. Metzenbaum of Ohio, when he said of the AK-47 semiautomatic rifle: "We know of only one instance in which this was used for hunting. When a psychopath in California went hunting for school children."[6]

In the end, gun control forces achieved an important goal in the Golden State. In March 1989, California became the first state to ban assault rifles. The law passed prohibits the sale, possession, or manufacture of military-style assault weapons. Citizens are now permitted to own such weapons only if the guns have been rendered inoperable.

New Jersey followed California's lead with its passage of stringent anti-assault weapon legislation in May 1990. New Jersey's bill allows owners of assault weapons one year to sell their guns out of state, surrender such weapons to police, or remove the guns' firing pins to render them inoperable.

Domestically, there have been some voluntary concessions on the part of gun manufacturers to assist in the effort to create safer urban environments. As early as March 15, 1989, Colt Industries agreed to suspend sales of its civilian look-alike copy of the M-16 rifle. Although the

AR-15 will continue to be sold to police and military customers, all sales to private customers have ceased. As a spokesperson for the weapon's manufacturer explained to the press: "We want to respond to the way the government is heading; sales suspension is obviously in the spirit of the decision on imports."[7]

However, gun control lobbyists have already pointed out what they regard as an unfortunate development abroad. They've made public the plans of some European manufacturers to circumvent the importation ban. For example, one German company has plans to shorten its semiautomatic rifles into semiautomatic pistols. Since the ban only covers rifles, these nearly-comparable lethal weapons could be legally imported and sold in the United States.

Nevertheless, gun control advocates have refused to become discouraged. Their continued pressure for federal legislation to nationally outlaw assault weapons has continued to mount. As a result, bills to ban the manufacture, sale, and possession of assault weapons have been introduced into both the House and the Senate.

In response to these developments, the NRA and other gun-lobbying groups have stressed that the snowballing demand for new antigun legislation is merely an outgrowth of media hysteria compounded by misinformation. An one gun shop owner from Pasadena, Texas, described the situation: "Our government has just reacted to panic and that is very foolish. They're going to pass a law against AK-47s because some idiot shot a bunch of kids when he could have done the same thing with a machete."[8]

Although the majority of the 70 million gun owners in America may be honest citizens, in recent times the NRA's firm opposition to even the most rudimentary weapon restrictions has been questioned by various segments of the population. People are beginning to ask exactly who needs a gun like the AK-47 assault rifle and for what purpose that weapon will be used.

Gun lobbyists have been criticized for what's been perceived as their failure to distinguish between the interests of the sportsman and the welfare of society as a whole. As one former FBI agent put it: "I can only hope the tide is turning.... [otherwise] law enforcement is eventually going to lose the domestic arms race."[9]

To some degree, the former FBI agent's wish may be quickly becoming reality as the public's support for gun control measures increases. According to a 1988 Gallup poll, 70 percent of those surveyed feel that the laws covering the sale of firearms should be tightened. However, perhaps it is comparably relevant that a 1989 *Time* CNN poll indicated that 84 percent of those queried firmly believe that they "have a right to own guns."[10]

In actuality, our nation may soon be faced with a perplexing dichotomy. Although there is rising sentiment for increased weapons regulation, an unprecedented number of Americans continue to purchase guns. A portion of these individuals may be intellectually in favor of gun control, but may emotionally cling to the notion of retaining a weapon for their own protection. As the continuing brutal intensity of urban violence results in increased demands for stricter controls, will many more American households be armed with guns they're reluctant to relinquish?

1. *Outdoor Life*, March 1986, p. 31.

2,3. Handgun Control, Inc. "What You Should Know About the Brady Bill."

4. *Time*, February 13, 1989, p. 41.

5. *The New York Times*, February 9, 1989, p. A26.

6. *The New York Times*, February 11, 1989, p. 6.

7. *The New York Times*, March 16, 1989, p. 23.

8,9. *Newsweek*, March 12, 1989, p. 29.

10. *Time*, February 27, 1989, p. 22.

F U R T H E R   R E A D I N G

BOOKS

Hawkes, Nigel. *Gun Control*. New York: Gloucester Press/Watts, 1988.

Hoobler, Dorothy, and Thomas Hoobler. *Drugs & Crime*. New York: Chelsea House, 1988.

Landau, Elaine. *Teenage Violence*. Englewood Cliffs, N.J.: Julian Messner, 1990.

Taubman, Bryna. *Lady Cop: True Stories of Policewomen in America's Toughest City*. New York: Warner Books, 1987.

Woods, Geraldine and Harold. *The Right to Bear Arms*. New York: Watts, 1986.

ARTICLES

"Bring Home a Friend." *Time*, Vol. 134, August 28, 1989, p. 15. National Rifle Association urges that discharged soldiers be allowed to import machine guns.

"Bush Embraces Gun Control in Crime Control." *American Rifleman*, Vol. 137, August 1989, p. 72. Comprehensive Violent Crime Control Act of 1989.

"Carnage Control." *Commonwealth*, Vol. 116, April 7, 1989, p. 195. Gun control in California.

"Effects of Curbs on Semiautomatic Guns Debated" by Charles Mohr. *The New York Times*, Vol. 138, March 16, 1989, p. A11.

"Florida Grandfather Charged Under New Child-Gun Law." *The New York Times*, Vol. 139, October 11, 1989, p. A13.

"Group Promotes St. Gabriel as a Patron of Handgun Owners." *National Catholic Reporter*, Vol. 23, May 22, 1987, p. 2.

"Have Weapons, Will Shoot: As the Toll Grows, a Survey Shows Americans Want to Crack Down" by Laurence I. Barrett. *Time*, Vol. 133, February 27, 1989, p. 22.

"Here We Stand" by J. Warren Cassidy. *American Rifleman*, Vol. 137, February 1989, p. 7. National Rifle Association action against gun control.

"Legislator Tunes into Foes of Guns" by Susan F. Rasky. *The New York Times*, Vol. 138, March 25, 1989, p. 8(N).

"Sarah Brady's Crusade; Fighting a Proposal to Ease Handgun Restrictions" by Mark Miller. *Newsweek*, Vol. 107, April 14, 1986, p. 22.

ORGANIZATIONS CONCERNED WITH FIREARMS

Citizens' Committee for the Right to Bear and Keep Arms
12500 N.E. Tenth Pl.
Liberty Park
Bellevue, WA 98005

Coalition to Stop Gun Violence
100 Maryland Avenue N.E.
Washington, D.C. 20002

Firearms Research and Identification Association
1608 Nogales Street, Suite 360
Rowland Heights, CA 91748

Foundation for Handgun Education
Box 72
110 Maryland Avenue N.E.
Washington, D.C. 20002

Gun Owners Inc.
5510 Birdcage, Suite 210
Citrus Heights, CA 95610

Handgun Control, Inc.
1400 K Street N.W.
Washington, D.C. 20005

National Association to Keep and Bear Arms
P.O. Box 78336
Seattle, WA 98178

National Rifle Association
1600 Rhode Island Avenue N.W.
Washington, D.C. 20036

Second Amendment Foundation
James Madison Bldg.
12500 N.E. Tenth Pl.
Bellevue, WA 98005

INDEX

ABOUT THE AUTHOR

Elaine Landau received her B.A. degree in English and journalism from New York University and a master's degree in Library and Information Science from Pratt Institute.

She has worked as a newspaper reporter, an editor, and a librarian but believes that many of her most exciting as well as rewarding hours have been spent researching and writing books for young people.

Ms. Landau lives in Sparta, New Jersey.